D0984230

WHEN BISHOPS MEET

WHEN BISHOPS MEET

An Essay Comparing Trent,

Vatican I, and Vatican II

JOHN W. O'MALLEY

THE BELKNAP PRESS OF

HARVARD UNIVERSITY PRESS

Cambridge, Massachusetts
London, England

2019

Copyright © 2019 by the President and Fellows of Harvard College
All rights reserved
Printed in the United States of America

FIRST PRINTING

Library of Congress Cataloging-in-Publication Data

Names: O'Malley, John W., author.
Title: When bishops meet : an essay comparing Trent, Vatican I, and
Vatican II / John W. O'Malley.
Description: Cambridge, Massachusetts : The Belknap Press of
Harvard University Press, 2019. | Includes bibliographical
references and index.
Identifiers: LCCN 2018059571 | ISBN 9780674988415 (alk. paper)
Subjects: LCSH: Councils and synods. | Council of Trent (1545–1563 :
Trento, Italy) | Vatican Council (1st : 1869–1870 : Basilica di San
Pietro in Vaticano) | Vatican Council (2nd : 1962–1965 : Basilica di
San Pietro in Vaticano) | Catholic Church—Government.
Classification: LCC BX825 .O43 2019 | DDC 262 / .52—dc23
LC record available at https://lccn.loc.gov/2018059571

For the Jesuits at Wolfington Hall

Contents

WHEN BISHOPS MEET

Introduction

Since 2008, I have published a monograph on each of the last three ecumenical councils of the Catholic church—the Council of Trent (1545–1563), Vatican Council I (1869–1870), and Vatican Council II (1962–1965). As I was writing them, I began to notice how similar they were in a number of ways, how different in others, and, most important, how the same three fundamental problems recurred in them. I began to see how one council's treatment of an issue threw light on how the others dealt with it. By the time I completed my book on Vatican Council I in 2018, I had decided to try my hand at a small book putting the three councils together, comparing and contrasting them. *When Bishops Meet* is the result.

The Council of Trent met in that small city because neither Catholics nor Protestants felt they could trust a council meeting in Rome or elsewhere in the Papal States. Due to the volatile political conditions of the time, it met in three distinct periods—1545–1547, 1551–1552, 1562–1563. Convoked to respond to Luther and other Protestants, it strove in its early stages to act as a reconciling agent with them. In time, however, it abandoned that hope and moved ahead simply to set the church on a better path, which resulted, among other things, in drawing a strong line of demarcation with the Protestant churches. In this way and others, the council had a lasting impact on modern Catholicism, even though it was often praised or damned for things it never did.

By the mid-nineteenth century, Catholics were ready to accept Rome as the site of the council that Pius IX (r. 1846–1878) convoked in 1869 to meet there. The pope, like most Catholic leaders, was deeply distressed over the utterly new situation ushered in by the French Revolution and saw it as destructive of Christian values and even of Western civilization itself. He saw an infallible pope as the remedy that could provide stability amid the threatening chaos. Papal infallibility became the dominating issue at the council, and it is for the council's definition of it that Vatican I is remembered.

A century later, Pope John XXIII (r. 1958–1963) convoked Vatican Council II. The convocation came as a great surprise because the persuasion had grown that Vatican I's definition of infallibility had rendered councils superfluous. Vatican II, like Vatican I, addressed the problem of the modern world, but a modern world much changed since 1869–1870. The prelates at the council realized that the church had to come to terms with that world and had to abandon, at least in some measure, its anti-world stance. The council is perhaps best understood in that perspective.

I base everything I say here about those three councils on what I said in the original books. On that level, there is nothing new in *When Bishops Meet*. On another, however, the book is altogether new. Putting issues side by side throws new and sometimes significant light on what might otherwise seem ho-hum information, such as the number of cardinals participating in a given council. The book thus provides new perspectives on each of the councils and, most important, new perspectives on councils as such.

The book is therefore unique. No book like it exists in any language regarding these councils, nor does any book like it exist in any language regarding other councils. *When Bishops Meet* therefore breaks new ground methodologically. It is a novel way of looking at councils and studying them—synchronically rather than, as usual, diachronically. Scholars have often pointed out individual instances of how one council might be like or different from another, but none has done a systematic and sustained analysis in any way resembling what I undertake here.

As the Table of Contents makes clear, I divide the book into three parts. In the first, I analyze the three most basic issues that explicitly or, more commonly, implicitly, concerned these councils: What is a council supposed to do? Does church teaching change? Who has final authority in the church? This is the part that provides important perspectives on the council phenomenon. In the second part, I analyze the changing roles of different categories of persons who participated in the councils. At Trent, for instance, laypersons were official members of the council and had direct influence on its proceedings, whereas at Vatican II their influence was, at best, indirect. In the third part, I ask the fundamental

question: Did these councils make any difference in
the Catholic church, in other churches, or in society
at large? I also speculate about what the future might
hold for councils.

When Bishops Meet is an extended essay on the
three councils. To some extent, it is an essay on Catholicism itself. As befits an essay, it is bereft of documentation supporting the points it makes. The
sweep of what I attempt here in so few pages makes
it virtually impossible to cite sources except in ways
that would satisfy no one. It leads me into generalizations that sometimes need serious qualification.
But the cause is not lost. Readers who want to know
how I arrived at what I say or at how I might qualify
it can consult my monographs on the councils, each
of which contains ample documentation and a full
index.

I stress, however, that *When Bishops Meet* stands
on its own. It is perfectly understandable without
any recourse to its parent texts. Persons who have
read one or more of those texts might better appre-
ciate what I say, but readers new to councils will
have no problem following the argument, learning
a lot about one of the most venerable institutions
of the Christian church, and, I hope, enjoying the
experience.

Councils trace their origins to the event related by Saint Luke in the fifteenth chapter of the Acts of the Apostles, where the evangelist described how "the apostles and elders" met in Jerusalem to decide what should be required of gentile converts to the new "way." With that unassailable precedent as a justification, similar meetings began to take place in the wider Hellenistic world as early as the second century wherever Christians were established in any number. The meetings took on common forms and adopted similar procedures. They were meetings, principally of bishops, who, because they were acting in Christ's name, had authority to make decisions binding on the church. The Greek name for them was synods, and the Latin name was councils. In the West both words came into use as synonyms and, until quite recently, were used interchangeably. Both the Council of Trent and Vatican II refer to themselves as synods.

THE HUNDREDS upon hundreds of local councils in the history of Christianity were extremely important, yet the twenty-one that Catholics generally consider ecumenical (church-wide) were more important still. They fall into two clearly distinct categories. Beginning with Nicaea in 325, the first eight were convoked by the Roman emperor or, in the case of Nicaea II in 787, by the Roman (Byzantine) empress. They were held in modern-day Turkey and were conducted in Greek. Bishops from the Latin church played small and usually insignificant roles in them. The bishop of Rome himself played roles ranging from marginal to important but never fully decisive.

Largely as a result of the Great Schism of 1054 in which leading prelates of the Greek-speaking and the Latin-speaking churches excommunicated one another, the West went its own way. The remaining thirteen councils were, therefore, all held in the West, were convoked by the pope, who invariably played a crucial role, and were conducted in Latin. In those regards, Trent and the two Vatican councils are similar.

They are similar, moreover, in another fundamental way. Each of them wrestled with the three fundamental issues mentioned earlier. These are issues so basic that they underlay more particular and sometimes more obvious issues that engaged the councils. They were the issues-under-the-issues. The first such issue was the literary forms or genres in which the councils expressed their decisions. Although this might seem a superficial or secondary issue, it is in fact the most important because it determines the kind of meeting a council will be and the goals it sets itself to accomplish. It answers two questions: What are we doing here? What do we want to accomplish?

The second is the problem of change. The church is by definition a conservative institution. Its reason for existence is to proclaim a message received long ago. If it fails in that proclamation, it has lost its identity. It cannot change or adulterate the message. Yet, the message is encased in human language and culture and thus is subject to some form of change, especially as it is transmitted through the centuries. How does the church remain faithful to the Gospel while at the same time consciously or unconsciously adapting it to be intelligible and appealing to contemporary men and women?

Simply put, does church teaching change? If so, in what way and to what degree in a given instance? When church practice is seen as closely or even remotely related to church teaching, it too can become a problem when it changes. Only when Europeans in the decades before the Council of Trent began to develop the discipline of philology and methods of textual criticism did they become keenly aware of discrepancies between past and present. The Council of Trent was, therefore, the first council in which change became a self-conscious issue. Change returned as an even more critical issue in the two subsequent councils.

The final issue-under-the-issues is the relationship of center to periphery, that is, the relationship between the papacy and the bishops, especially bishops gathered in council. At stake here is not only how a council functions when presided over by the pope but the larger question of how the church itself is governed. To put the question more specifically, Is the Catholic tradition of church governance hierarchical or collegial—or both?

The question leads naturally into Part Two, on the participants in the councils. Bishops are the constants as participants and as decision-makers—councils are by definition meetings of bishops. In the long history of councils, however, other categories of persons have played key and sometimes decisive roles, and in other instances some who held crucial roles in one council were virtually absent from others. Only when councils are placed side by side do such important discrepancies clearly emerge.

We assume councils were important and had an impact. In Part Three, I examine that assumption and also speculate on the future. I offer some considerations about the impact of the three councils, suggest how it differed from one to another, and point out how difficult it is to assess a council's impact satisfactorily. Finally, out comes my crystal ball as I try to look into the future in answer to a question I am often asked, "When will there be a Vatican III?"

That is what this book is all about and how it is put together. I think you will find it an easy read, and I hope you will find it a pleasant one. If you persevere, I know you will find it informative—a read that will teach you a lot about the Catholic church and give you helpful perspectives on the state of Catholicism today. It also might help you think in a new way about other institutions in which you are involved.

PART ONE

Three Great Issues

I

What Do Councils Do?

Beginning in the earliest centuries of Christianity, councils adopted forms and procedures based on those in use in the secular institutions of their day, and they continued to use them until Vatican II, though of course with modifications and adaptations as circumstances required. The forms gave councils their structure and determined their goals. The Council of Trent inherited the traditional pattern and for the most part conformed to it. It made at least one significant modification, which Vatican I without second thought adopted. Then came Vatican II. With only vague intimations of how radical they were being, the prelates at Vatican II completely abandoned the traditional forms and introduced a new one. With that, they broke with almost two thousand years of history and redefined what a council is supposed to do. They made Vatican II a council like no other.

The Council of Nicaea

By the second century, councils had already become one of Christianity's most characteristic institutions. As they spread in the Hellenistic world, adapting as a matter of course and almost by osmosis common procedural models, they looked to the Roman Senate. The Senate made laws. It also rendered verdicts of guilt or innocence on persons accused of high-level crimes against the state and thus acted as a court of criminal justice.

This development culminated and received paradigmatic form with the first church-wide council, the Council of Nicaea, 325. The role of Emperor Constantine at it strengthened the analogy between councils and the Senate. The emperor had moved the imperial capital from Rome to Constantinople (present-day Istanbul), and he convoked the council to meet under his watchful eye in his palace in nearby Nicaea. He in large measure set the agenda for the council, viz., the resolution of the doctrinal controversy set in motion by Arius, a priest from Alexandria who denied the full divinity of Christ.

The emperor convoked the council as the first step in his efforts to restore good public order in the empire, which especially in the East had been badly disrupted by the Arian controversy. He opened the council with a welcoming speech, and he presided over some of the council's sessions as its honorary president. He assured the bishops that he would himself enforce their decisions. The law of the council became the law of the empire. Even so, the bishops had direct control of the meeting. Their goal was the restoration of doctrinal order in the church, a goal coterminous with the emperor's.

To accomplish their task, the bishops did what the Senate would do. They heard the case against Arius and found him guilty of propagating heresy. As they put it in their "Letter to the Egyptians," they had "unanimously agreed that anathemas be pronounced against his impious opinions and his blasphemous terms."

In subsequent centuries, councils continued to condemn persons convicted by them of propagating heresy. The most notorious such case was the condemnation of Jan Hus at the Council of Constance

(1414–1418), which resulted in his being turned over to "the secular arm" to be burned at the stake, an event that makes devastatingly clear that councils acted as courts of criminal justice.

Although the bishops at Nicaea took the case against Arius as the major business of the council, they used the occasion to settle other matters that had come to their attention. They made laws regarding certain behaviors, with penalties attached for nonobservance. They, for instance, levied penalties against clerics who castrated themselves, they forbade admitting to the clergy converts from paganism until they had undergone a period of testing, and they strictly forbade clergy to bring a woman to live in their household unless she were their mother or sister. They passed other decrees making similar regulations concerning clerical discipline. In later centuries, such decrees were sometimes called reform decrees.

The juridical genre the council used to formulate its decrees was the canon, a generally short ordinance proscribing or prescribing certain behaviors, with penalties attached for nonobservance. Literary genres produce styles of expression peculiar to themselves, which include vocabulary appropriate for the genre. The language of canons was terse, straightforward, without literary adornment, and often technical—language appropriate for laws.

But Nicaea also published a profession of faith, which is a different genre. It is not a law as such, but, as the word itself indicates, a proclamation or assertion. In this case, the council fathers introduced a philosophical term, substance. They saw the introduction of this nonbiblical term as necessary in order to express unambiguously the orthodox Christological doctrine as distinct from that of Arius. Councils increasingly felt constrained to make use of such terms in order to obviate misunderstandings of what they were saying.

Nicaea set patterns for the future. Subsequent councils passed laws, some of which pertained to behavior regarding doctrine and some to other aspects of behavior in the church. Thus emerged the classic distinction between doctrinal and disciplinary ("reform") decrees. Even the doctrinal decrees were, however, often formulated in canons, and therefore were laws. As laws they dealt with observable behavior, not with motivation or conscience: "If anyone should *say* such and such—or *teach* or *preach* such and such—let him be anathema," not "If anyone should *believe* or *think* such and such."

Anathema was a pronouncement of excommunication, a very severe penalty for a Christian.

Such decrees therefore almost inevitably carried a penalty for nonobservance. They were not exhortations. Once universities began to train canon lawyers in the early years of the thirteenth century, juridical terms began to appear more frequently in council documents, play a more important role in them, and bear a more technical meaning. As the universities began at the same time to train professional philosophers and theologians, technical terms derived from those disciplines began to appear more frequently. Thus, the resulting decrees generally required experts to interpret them.

Early on, therefore, councils came to be meetings of a certain kind. They were legislative and judicial meetings, and their function was to promote good order in the church—good order in doctrinal behavior and good order in other aspects of behavior. Although councils over the course of the centuries made use of a wide variety of literary forms, such as confessions of faith, bulls, letters, instructions, and constitutions, canons emerged as the genre councils most frequently, consistently, and characteristically employed to accomplish their goals. In this regard, Nicaea once again set the pattern by issuing twenty.

The next ecumenical council, Constantinople I, 381, issued seven, and then Ephesus, 431, issued twelve. The entire corpus of Lateran Councils I, II, and III, the first Western councils, is made up entirely of canons. The Council of Trent issued over 250.

The Council of Trent

The rapid spread of Lutheranism catalyzed Emperor Charles V (r. 1519–1556) and Pope Paul III (r. 1534–1549) into forming an uneasy partnership that resulted in the pope convening the Council of Trent. Luther's challenge was both doctrinal and disciplinary. His doctrine was encapsulated in the following triad: faith alone, grace alone, Scripture alone. Although that triad might bear an interpretation consonant with Catholic orthodoxy, as elaborated by Luther it not only sounded heterodox but had led him to radical conclusions about the number and definition of the sacraments. Luther had to be answered.

In his "Appeal to the German Nobility," 1520, Luther took on the role of a church reformer by denouncing abuses in the church and especially in the practices of the Roman curia, such as the lavish lifestyle of the cardinals. In so doing, he certainly did not stand alone. Since the Council of Constance, church reform had become almost an obsession with seriously minded Christians. Luther's call for reform of church discipline was special, however, in its provocative formulation, in the controversial theological principles that undergirded it, and in the great furor that accompanied it. In this regard, too, he had to be answered.

Contrary to what is commonly thought, Pope Paul III did not convoke the council to condemn Luther. He yielded to the desire of Charles V that the council try to find a way to reconcile with "the reformers." Although Paul was highly skeptical that on a doctrinal plane a reconciliation was feasible, he was at least for the moment willing to suspend his disbelief. That willingness led to a little noticed but significant change from how past councils had often proceeded. Paul informed the council shortly after it opened that it was to condemn whatever was wrong in the teachings of "the Lutherans," but not condemn the persons to whom the teachings were ascribed.

The council acted accordingly. In contrast with previous councils, it condemned "anyone" who taught such and such, but named no names. When during the second of the council's three periods (1551–1552), a few Lutherans accepted the invitation to come to the council to present their case, the council assured them again and again that they would suffer no harm to their persons. Thus it came about that the Council of Trent, though it condemned doctrines it attributed to "the Lutherans," did not act as a judicial body levying sentences against specific individuals.

As a legislative body, however, Trent emerged as one of the most prodigal in the history of the church, as is suggested by the large number of canons it issued. Yet, an important part of the Tridentine corpus is purely instructional. Most of the doctrinal texts, for instance, have two distinct parts. They open with "chapters," which provided a positive presentation of Catholic teaching. The chapters are then followed by canons that condemned heterodox versions of that teaching. While Trent was certainly not the first council to contain instructional or exhortatory genres, it was especially important because of the deliberate and consistent way it went about it. In adopting this way of proceeding, as well as in abstaining from condemning individuals, the council, while still largely conforming to the legislative-judicial model, represented a qualification of it.

Especially in the first period (1545–1547), the fathers at Trent tried to present the belief of the church as far as possible in biblical and patristic terms, but they soon discovered that they could not accurately express themselves without having recourse to Scholastic categories. Those categories become more prominent once the council addressed the sacraments. As might be expected, juridical language abounded in the council's reform decrees.

Vatican I

More than three centuries elapsed between Trent and Vatican I. In response to the new political, social, and cultural situations resulting from the French Revolution and its Pan-European Napoleonic aftermath, Pius IX decided to convoke a council, which he announced on June 29, 1868. He established commissions to prepare materials for it. The commissions came up with an extensive agenda that covered both doctrinal and disciplinary issues, most of which had arisen in the wake of these new situations that created the reality that came to be known as "the modern world."

The seizure of Rome on September 20, 1870, by the forces of the new Kingdom of Italy cut the council short, so that it was able to deal with only two issues, both of them doctrinal. The council's dogmatic constitution, *Dei Filius,* dealt with the relationship between faith and reason, a response to modern rationalism and atheism. Its other constitution, *Pastor Aeternus,* defined the doctrines of papal primacy and papal infallibility, a response in the first place to bishop-centered ecclesiologies such as Gallicanism but also a response to the political instability brought on by liberty, equality, and fraternity. A large number of Catholic laymen and clerics believed that a strong papal monarchy was the only institution that could restore order to society.

Because three centuries had intervened since the convocation of Trent by Paul III, the memory of how such meetings functioned had dimmed. To discover how to proceed, the preparatory commissions sought precedents, and they in the first instance looked to the decrees published by Trent. Like most of the doctrinal decrees of Trent, therefore, both *Dei Filius* and *Pastor Aeternus* began with chapters and concluded with canons.

Although the canons attached to *Dei Filius* had a broader scope, they were more specifically directed against three German Catholic philosophers / theologians who were considered "semi-rationalists"— Anton Günther, Georg Hermes, and Jakob Froschhammer. *Pastor Aeternus* had a similarly broad scope but directed one canon specifically against Bishop Henri Maret, a participant in the council. As at Trent, however, the canons mentioned no names. Vatican I was virtually unique among councils in having no disciplinary decrees, even though such decrees were foreseen by the preparatory commissions. The abrupt suspension of the council after the seizure of Rome meant that they were never addressed. Nonetheless, Vatican I was, like Trent, a legislative, judicial, and instructional institution.

Vatican II

When Pope John XXIII announced on January 25, 1959, his intention to convoke a council, he mentioned almost in passing two aims for it—to promote "the enlightenment, edification, and joy of the entire Christian people" and to extend a "cordial invitation to the faithful of the separated communities to participate with us in this quest for unity and grace." Although tantalizingly vague, both aims are remarkable for being unqualifiedly positive.

In his address on October 11, 1962, opening the council, the pope underscored the positive approach he wanted the council to take when he told the assembled prelates to avoid condemnations and "make use of the medicine of mercy rather than severity." With those simple words, the pope liberated the council from the legislative-judicial model and set in motion a process that led the council to abandon the most characteristic function councils had performed up to that time, consolidating public order in the church and isolating it from external contamination. He gave the council freedom to do something new. He gave the council freedom to *be* something new.

The bishops heard the message, and from the very first moment they set about implementing it. To say something positive rather than negative means praising it rather than criticizing or condemning it. Praise is therefore the major rhetorical form the council adopted. Praise language is different from legislative-judicial language.

At Vatican II, the language issue, largely implicit in Trent and Vatican I, burst open upon the floor of Saint Peter's in the first intervention on the council's first working day on the first document the council addressed, *Sacrosanctum Concilium*, "On the Sacred Liturgy." Cardinal Joseph Frings of Cologne commented, "The draft is to be commended for its modest and truly pastoral style, full of the spirit of Holy Scripture and the Fathers of the

Church." The style issue recurred again and again in interventions until it became clear that the council was set for a change in the traditional language, which entailed a change in literary genre.

The total absence of canons in the council's final documents is the first clue that something of significance had taken place. The absence is even more remarkable when placed in relationship to the Roman Synod of 1960, which was seen at the time as a dress rehearsal for the council. The synod issued 755 canons for the diocese of Rome, principally on clerical discipline. Vatican II, which concluded just five years later, issued not a single one. Its literary form and thus its positive approach virtually precluded canons, which almost by definition entailed punitive measures for nonobservance.

Instead of proscribing and prescribing, Vatican II by means of praise held up ideals. Instead of proscribing and prescribing, it held up norms. The sixteen final documents of the council are committee documents, and as such lack the polish single authorship might provide. They are complex and cannot be reduced to one literary form. Nonetheless, their consistently positive language removes them from a legislative-judicial form of discourse and for the most part places them in a panegyric form.

The transformation of genre had profound repercussions, perhaps more profound than its authors realized and certainly more profound than most commentators on the council subsequently grasped. The consistent employment of the panegyric genre resulted in a shift in councils' goals. It resulted in a redefinition of what a council is. As modeled in Vatican II, a council is a meeting in which the church takes time out to explore its identity, to recall and develop its most precious values, and to proclaim to the world its sublime vision for humanity. This is new. This is a paradigm shift.

At Vatican II the council remained a meeting, principally of bishops, that made decisions binding on the church. But the decisions consisted principally in providing normative values and ideals to guide persons in their choices and mode of life. The decisions were less intent on preventing crimes and curbing misbehavior and more intent on providing encouragement for persons' best instincts and aspirations.

The ideals the council proposed had institutional implications. The second chapter of *Lumen Gentium,* the dogmatic constitution "On the Church," holds up the ideal of the church as "the people of God" and thus expresses the participatory role all members are expected to play in every aspect of the church's life. The ideals thus had a strong instructional character.

Like preceding councils, Vatican II wanted to secure public order in the church, and it does so in many of its directives. But the directives are for the most part norms that carry with them no punishment for nonobservance. The lack of punishment does not mean the directives are not prescriptive. On the contrary, they are professed with the full authority of the council and thus cannot be shrugged off as suggestions.

Like previous councils, Vatican II also wanted to protect the church from contamination, but it now saw "the Other" more as potential partner than enemy, more an object of reconciliation than alienation, less as a danger than as a potential enhancement. It saw encounters with the Other as a stimulus to reflection upon its own identity and as an occasion for deeper appreciation of it.

When the panegyric genre predominated in a council decree, something even further was at stake. The goal of panegyric is enhancement of appreciation for a worthy or beautiful object. Panegyric wants to touch the soul and inspire it to embrace an ideal. It wants to inculcate values. Vatican II thus moved beyond enforcing certain kinds of behavior to inspiring holy yearnings. No wonder that holiness became a leitmotif of the council, playing a role unmentioned in previous councils.

Previous councils legislated to compel certain behaviors—"Do this. Don't do that." They did not venture into people's interior life. For any institution such regulations are essential for securing order and making it possible for people to live and work together. Vatican II, however, moved beyond behavior modification to motivation and inspiration, and for that reason conscience, a subject that like holiness was never mentioned in previous councils, emerged as an important theme at Vatican II.

In its general orientation, as expressed especially in its most characteristic vocabulary, Vatican II devised a profile of the ideal Christian. A dominant feature in that profile was the yearning for reconciliation with the Other as much as possible. Panegyric is by definition a reconciling mode of discourse because it praises and highlights what is praiseworthy in the Other and gives it a new force and actuality. From the rhetoric of praise and congratulation resulted the reconciling dynamic that animated the council and that found expression in a variety of important ways.

The council reconciled the relationship between bishops and pope in its instillation of collegiality in its decree on the church. The council reconciled the church with non-Western cultures in its decree on the liturgy, with other Christians in its decree on ecumenism, with non-Christian religions in its decree on that subject, with nonbelievers in its decree on the church in the modern world, and with the modern world itself in that same decree. The council thus defined the church as essentially a reconciling institution. This was not a new idea or ideal, but the council gave it a breadth, a power, a clarity, and a dominance it had not had before.

If this was an ideal and pressing value for the church, it was the same for members of the church, and for no one more so than for the popes. Beginning with Pope Paul VI at the time of the council and down to the present, the popes have emerged as the most prominent and most respected voice for peoples of all faiths and no faith, as each of them pleaded for peace, reconciliation, compassion, and the end of violence in a world desperately in need of such a voice.

The vocabulary employed by the documents of Vatican II is strikingly positive, especially when compared with previous councils. Although the words can be divided into categories such as horizontal words, equality words, reciprocity words, and empowerment words, they evince an emotional kinship among themselves and, along with the genre in which they are encased, express an overall orientation and coherence in values.

Among such words are brothers and sisters, friendship, cooperation, collaboration, partnership, collegiality, freedom, dialogue, servant, dignity, and holiness. Among such words is conscience. Absent is the word anathema and its equivalents. Absent is the word monarchy, so often used earlier to describe the church. The legislative-judicial model imposed obedience to external authority, whereas Vatican II shifts the focus to a higher authority, an interior authority:

Deep within their consciences, men and women discover a law that they have not laid upon themselves but that they must obey. Its voice, ever calling them to love and to do what is good and avoid what is evil, tells them inwardly at the right moment: do this, shun that.

For they have a law in their hearts inscribed by God. Their dignity lies in observing this law, and by it they will be judged. . . . By conscience the law is made known in a wonderful way that is fulfillment in love for God and for one's neighbor. Through loyalty to conscience, Christians are joined with others in the search for truth and for the right solutions to the many moral problems that arise both in the lives of individuals and in social relationships. (*Gaudium et Spes,* number 16)

No previous council was capable of such a statement because it would have been foreign to its literary genre. In the Christian tradition, conscience has always been the ultimate norm that an individual must obey, but the genre of previous councils inhibited them from saying it.

The values these words express are anything but new in the Christian tradition. They are as common in Christian discourse, or more common, than their opposites. To say the least, however, they are not at all common in councils. Vatican II did not invent the words or imply that they were not already operative in the church. Yet, taken as a whole, they convey the sweep of a newly and forcefully expressed style of life for individual Christians and for the church as an institution. The Second Vatican Council held up for admiration and actualization the values the words expressed.

To dismiss the vocabulary as simply a pastoral ploy is to fail to understand that the vocabulary serves as the expression of the dynamism of a quite specific literary form. Councils must express themselves with words. To change the words is to change the form. To change the form is to create something different from what prevailed before. To change to something different from what earlier prevailed is to change the nature of the object in question. It gives the object a new definition. That is what happened at Vatican II. The style change resulted in a council so different from all those that preceded it that it cannot be fully understood without applying to it different interpretative principles, the first of which is taking account of the literary genre the council employed.

Vatican II is the most complex council in the history of the church by reason of the international perspective it adopted, by reason of its awareness of the radical cultural changes that confronted it, and by reason of the number and difficulty of the issues it chose to address. Its adoption of a new genre to express itself adds to the complexity and to the difficulty in interpreting it in the full breadth of its significance. Taking account of the genre is, however, the first and most essential interpretative principle required to unlock that significance. When that principle is employed, it reveals that Vatican II is a council so unlike any other that it redefined what a council is because it redefined what a council does.

What, then, is a council? The original definition stands, a meeting principally of bishops gathered in Christ's name to make decisions binding on the church. But with Vatican II the nature of the decisions changed. Vatican II thus became, I repeat, a meeting in which the church explored and articulated anew its identity, recalled and developed its most precious values, and proclaimed to the world its sublime vision for humanity.

2

Does Church Teaching Change?

Although the documents of the early councils of the church recognized that bad customs and bad teaching had to be uprooted, which is a form of change, they most characteristically betray a sense of continuity with previous Christian teaching and practice. They called for continuation and implementation of ancient customs and ancient traditions—*antiqua lex, antiqua traditio.*

The documents of the medieval councils very much follow the same pattern. Although they in fact deal with the twists and turns in culture and institutional structures of their day, they lack a keen sense of discrepancy between past and present, and thus the councils never felt the necessity to address the discrepancy directly. Only with the Italian Renaissance of the fifteenth century and then the Reformation early in the next century did this ahistorical mind-set receive its first serious challenges. The Council of Trent was, therefore, the first council that had to take those challenges into account.

The Council of Trent

Luther saw his doctrine of justification by faith alone as the very core of the Gospel message. To reject it was to reject Christianity itself. As he began to experience hostility from the church hierarchy and from theologians concerning his teaching, he concluded that the church had not only failed to proclaim the Gospel but had proclaimed its antithesis, the heresy of justification by good works. The church had betrayed the teaching of Christ and had thereby ceased being the true church. In the course of the centuries, the church had changed, Luther maintained, and changed radically for the worse. Between it and the congregation of Christian faithful founded by Christ yawned a gap of many centuries. The church of his day was discontinuous with the teaching of Christ and the apostles.

When the bishops convened at Trent in 1545, they soon realized that justification was the key doctrinal issue at stake. After seven months of sometimes acrimonious discussion, they were finally able to articulate a statement that won their overwhelming approval. Neither at this nor at any other point did the council explicitly discuss whether the church had failed to proclaim the true doctrine. The prelates at Trent assumed that church teaching was continuous with the teaching of the Gospel, and they therefore simply affirmed or implied that what they taught was orthodox and true to the tradition.

In the early twentieth century, the important English historian and philosopher R. G. Collingwood designated this style of historical thinking "substantialism," and he saw it as the chief defect of the ancient Roman historians. Livy, for instance, took for granted that Rome was an unchanging substance that sailed through the sea of the centuries without being affected by it. Christian thinkers inherited this tradition and without examining it applied it to the church.

By the time of the council, however, an awareness of living in particularly evil times gripped many Europeans. Their times were the worst of all, the low point in a long process of decline from a purer and more authentic past. The church, they believed, was not exempt from this process. For Catholics and especially for the bishops gathered at Trent, the upheavals in the wake of the Reformation confirmed and exacerbated the awareness of a pervasive darkness. On at least three occasions, the bishops at the council lamented how calamitous were the times in which the council was taking place. They therefore accepted the idea of change for the worse, but they did not see it applying to doctrine, which somehow was immune to the historical process.

They did see change as applying to the discipline of "the clergy and the Christian people." The expression implies that the morals and mores of the people living within the institution of the church had declined, but not the institution itself, and most certainly not its doctrine. The documents of Trent rest, therefore, on an operative distinction between the church and its members. The former exists unchanged and apart from the contingencies to which the members are subject.

The council directed its changes therefore to the members, especially the clergy who occupied the three official pastoral offices in the church—pope, bishop, pastor of parishes. In trying to enforce changes in the behavior of officeholders, the council did not see itself as innovating but, rather, as restoring former norms and practices.

What was required to counter the evils of the age was a recovery and restoration of the healthy ecclesiastical discipline of the past. The reforms of Trent for the most part consisted, therefore, in strengthening or significantly reformulating older canonical regulations, especially as those regulations related to the clergy. The council restored, revived, and called back into operation the good norms of the past—*restituere, innovare, revocare.*

In actual fact, however, the council made changes that were innovations, not simply a burnishing of past laws. The decree *Tametsi* is the clearest example of such innovations. It stipulated that henceforth the church would consider no marriage valid unless witnessed by a priest. The council intended the decree to stamp out the abuse of so-called clandestine marriages, that is, the exchange of vows between the two partners with no witness present. Such marriages made it possible for one of the spouses, usually the man, to deny later that a marriage had taken place and to abandon his wife and, often, his children.

There was no precedent for *Tametsi* in the entire history of the church, a fact of which the bishops at Trent were aware. They were aware, therefore, that sometimes measures had to be adopted that were real changes from past practice and standards of behavior. The debate at Trent on *Tametsi* was heated, however, because it did not concern merely sacramental practice but seemed to have doctrinal implications.

The problem was this: If the consent of the spouses constituted the sacrament, which everybody agreed was the case, how could the church legitimately declare a consented-to union invalid? Did the church have the right and the authority to impose a condition on the validity of marriages that intruded on the partners' exchange of vows, the constitutive element of the sacrament? How could the church declare invalid in the future marriages that in the past it had recognized as valid, even if forbidden? The bishops discussed these objections and somehow came to the conclusion that they could pass the decree. At Trent, therefore, the problem of doctrinal change lurked in the shadows, poised to strike in the open at any moment.

But when Trent treated doctrine directly, it spoke clearly and declared, "No change!" It reformed mores, but it "confirmed" doctrine. In reaction to Luther, no previous council ever insisted as explicitly or implied so regularly that the present teaching of the church was identical with that of the apostolic age and that there had been no change in it in the intervening centuries. When the council affirmed that in the Catholic church "the ancient, absolute, and in every respect perfect faith and doctrine" of the Eucharist had been retained unchanged, it was only making explicit for one of its doctrinal pronouncements what underlay them all.

Vatican I

In Italy by the middle of the fifteenth century, new critical methods for dealing with historical texts had developed. The Italian humanist Lorenzo Valla led the way. In his *Adnotationes in Novum Testamentum,* he showed how the Latin Vulgate failed in many instances to convey the sense of the original Greek text, and through philological criticism he showed that the document known as "The Donation of Constantine" was a forgery. With these works Valla founded the discipline of philology and in so doing gave impetus to a newly keen sense of anachronism. He thus sowed the seeds of what developed into modern historical consciousness.

The critical approach to historical texts and to the past that Valla and later humanists such as Erasmus pioneered caught on, gained momentum, and reached a culminating turning point in the nineteenth century. It was a century in which awareness of historical change began conditioning scholars' approach to virtually every text in every discipline, including sacred texts. It was, moreover, the century of Darwin's *On the Origin of Species.* Evolution, development, progress, change—these words marked the culture of the age.

The Enlightenment of the eighteenth century had largely rejected any role for the past in prescribing norms for the present, and it had thrown history's goal into the future. The liberal philosophies of the nineteenth century assumed that progress was inevitable in virtually every aspect of human life and endeavor. The world moved forward in a process of change for the better, as Darwin showed. To the delight of some and to the horror of others, Darwin seemed to reduce the story of Adam and Eve to a naïve fable.

The Bible as well as the history of the church now came under newly skeptical criticism in the universities, which revived in the nineteenth century after a long period of stagnation. Germany was the revival's epicenter, most especially the University of Berlin. Sharpening the methods pioneered by Renaissance humanists, Leopold von Ranke trained generations of talented students in rigorous methods of historical analysis and textual criticism.

This development, long in the making, moved the discipline of history from its former base in rhetoric and moral philosophy to more controlled methods of research, which at a certain point began to be described as scientific. The methods professed objectivity in evaluating evidence and freedom from contamination by apologetic concerns. They likewise professed freedom from what the maintenance of received opinions might require. For professional historians, these methods spelled the end of substantialism. Every historical reality had a history. Simply by being historical, each and every historical reality changed—at least to some degree. As did other scholars of the era, Catholic exegetes and historians felt the impact of such methods and had to reckon with them. At Vatican I in that regard, Catholic bishops had to deal with historical objections to the doctrine of papal infallibility, that is, the pope's prerogative to declare with absolute finality that a truth is divinely revealed and must be believed by all faithful Catholics.

When on June 26, 1867, Pius IX made known to bishops and pilgrims present in Rome his intention to convoke a council, he described its purpose in the most general terms: to review the problems facing the church and to find appropriate remedies for them. He established commissions to prepare the agenda, which resulted in a wide range of topics for the council to deal with. Among those topics, however, was none dealing with the popes' infallibility. But because the Catholic press, especially in France, had carried on such a vigorous campaign for it before the council opened, the early emergence of infallibility at the council as the issue that would dominate it was almost inevitable.

A sizeable minority of bishops coming especially from Germany, Austria, and Hungary opposed defining the doctrine and based their objections in large part on historical grounds. According to those bishops, the doctrine lacked historical foundation in the church's doctrine and in the church's practice. According to them also, there were instances where a pope had taught a heterodox opinion. Among those most adamantly opposed to infallibility on such grounds was Karl-Josef Hefele, bishop of Rottenburg, who had already published several volumes of his highly respected history of the councils.

Leaders of the majority at the council tried to show, however, that the supposed instances of papal fallibility could be explained or were irrelevant. The assumption that the church and especially its teachings did not change had by the nineteenth century become axiomatic in most Catholic circles, which to some extent was the legacy of the Council of Trent. According to this assumption, the present church related to the past through a bond of virtually unqualified continuity.

In this mode of thinking, historical arguments were irrelevant in the face of seemingly irrefutable texts from Scripture or later documents of the church. The abstract and ahistorical method of the Scholastic system of theology further helped shield doctrine from historical contingency. A historical naiveté that took the present situation as the norm for interpreting the past and that projected present practice and understanding onto it also contributed to this substantialistic mode of thinking.

The clearest statement of the majority's stance on the matter occurred in the *Relatio* (explanatory notes) that accompanied the first draft of the infallibility decree:

As has without exception been shown above from the most important texts [*monumentis*], the infallibility of the Roman Pontiff is a truth divinely revealed. Therefore, it is impossible that it can ever be proved false by any historical facts. If, however, such facts are brought forward to oppose it, they must themselves be deemed false insofar as they seem opposed.

In their wording, neither of the council's two decrees—*Dei Filius* and *Pastor Aeternus*—directly engaged with the historical issues that were germane to them, but the statement in the *Relatio* reveals the mind-set that underlay them. Although Vatican Council I shut its eyes to the problem of change, the problem did not go away. It exploded onto the scene with the Modernist crisis some decades later.

In the late nineteenth century, advocacy among Catholics of a sometimes undiscriminating adoption of the new historical approach to sacred texts and sacred doctrines became part of the amorphous phenomenon known as Modernism. The inclusiveness of the seemingly all-encompassing label "Modernism" suggests why it is difficult to find a common thread linking so-called Modernists to one another beyond their desire to help the church reconcile itself with what they thought was best in intellectual culture as it had evolved into the present. However, a general though not universally accepted premise of the movement (if it can be called that) was the pervasiveness of change and the need to come to terms with it.

The storm broke on July 3, 1907. On that day, the Holy Office issued the decree *Lamentabili* condemning sixty-five propositions supposedly held by the Modernists. Two months later, Pope Pius X (r. 1903–1914) followed up with his encyclical *Pascendi Dominici Gregis.* For the sweep of its accusations, the accusatory style of its language, and the severity of its provisions, *Pascendi* had few, if any, precedents in the annals of the modern papacy. A veritable purge followed, which, besides the damage it did to Catholic intellectual life, confirmed among many Catholics an already pervasive readiness to ignore change. The Catholic church, it was often proudly said, does not change.

Vatican II

Despite the severe measures taken by the Holy See against exegetes and church historians accused of being Modernists, a relatively small but well-trained number of Catholic scholars in the early decades of the twentieth century continued to apply historical modes of research and analysis to ecclesiastical texts and to problems in church practice. As surveillance over such scholars diminished, their numbers grew and their methods began to receive a positive or at least tolerant reception. When in 1943 Pope Pius XII published his encyclical *Divino Afflante Spiritu,* he validated historical and archeological methods for the study of the Bible, which was an implicit validation of similar approaches for other areas of sacred studies. Bit by bit, scholars began to show that every aspect of church life and teaching had been affected by change.

For winning acceptance of the idea that change affected even doctrine, no book was more important than John Henry Newman's *Essay on the Development of Christian Doctrine,* published in 1845. The book appeared, therefore, fourteen years before Darwin's *On the Origin of Species.* Like Darwin's work, it reflected the preoccupation of the age with evolution, development, progress, and the implications of the historical process.

By using different analogies, Newman showed how teachings evolved while remaining true to their origins. Teachings were both continuous and discontinuous with their earlier articulation. The book, still the classic in the field, put the problem of change in doctrine on the stage of theological discourse to a degree unknown before. Although published well before Vatican Council I, it had no significant impact on the council's debates, but in the decades leading up to Vatican II most Catholic bishops and theologians accepted its basic premise in some form or other.

In France in the middle of the nineteenth century Prosper Guéranger, abbot of the monastery of Solesmes, set in motion a movement in which critical methods were applied to liturgical texts. By the middle of the next century liturgical scholars were calling for changes in how the liturgy was celebrated to bring it more into conformity with what they saw as its true character, which had been obscured by accretions through the centuries. Pope Pius XII responded to them in part through two decrees, in 1951 and 1955, in which he completely reorganized the liturgies for the last three days of Holy Week to bring them in line with liturgists' recommendations.

The stage had thus been set for Vatican II to take a stance on the problem of change radically different from that of the two previous councils. The bishops and theologians at the council accepted the reality of change as a matter of course. Their only questions were about how to explain it, about how far it could legitimately go, and what the criteria were for making changes.

Change—the word appeared in the first sentence of the first paragraph of the first document the council published, *Sacrosanctum Concilium,* "On the Sacred Liturgy." The sentence stated that the council intended to adapt to contemporary conditions those aspects of the liturgy that were subject to change *(mutatio). Sacrosanctum Concilium* thus sounded the first note in what was to be an underlying and pervasive issue at the council.

This keener sense of historical change took three forms in the council, captured in three words current at the time—*aggiornamento* (Italian for updating or modernizing), development (an unfolding or evolution, sometimes the equivalent of progress), and *ressourcement* (French for a return to the sources). A basic assumption undergirded the council's employment of these three modes in which change might take place: The Catholic tradition was richer, broader, and more malleable than often perceived in the past. The bishops who appropriated that assumption did so not as an abstract truth but as a license to undertake a thorough examination of the status quo. They reacted against interpretations of Catholic doctrine and practice that reduced it to simplistic and ahistorical formulae. They reacted against substantialism.

Of the three terms, interpreters of the council and especially the popular media most often invoked *aggiornamento* to explain what Vatican II was all about. The term, generally attributed to Pope John XXIII, equivalently occurred in his charge to the council in his opening address, in which he told the fathers of the council to make "appropriate changes" *(opportunis emendationibus)* that would help the church in its pastoral mission.

In principle, *aggiornamento* was nothing new. The church had perforce always adapted to new situations. In recent times, the Vatican adopted microphones and amplifiers before the House of Commons and typewriters before the British Foreign Office. But in at least four regards the *aggiornamento* of Vatican II was new. First, some of the changes made in its name touched upon things ordinary Catholics assumed were normative, such as Latin liturgy, and hence they had a startling impact. Second, no previous council had taken *aggiornamento* as a broad principle rather than as a rare exception.

Third, the *aggiornamento* of Vatican II related not to modern inventions or polite conventions of society but to certain cultural assumptions and values of "the modern world," the most basic of which, such as liberty, equality, and fraternity, stemmed most directly from the Enlightenment. These were assumptions and values that Vatican Council I implicitly rejected and, hence, the *aggiornamento* of Vatican II marked a turn in the road. Fourth, the broad adoption of deliberate reconciliation of the church with certain changes taking place outside it provided an entry point for a more dynamic understanding of how the church functioned.

Dynamism was even more relevant to the concept of development, which was by definition a movement—a movement to a further point along a given path. It was a cumulative though sometimes also a pruning process by which the tradition of the church became richer or perhaps clearer than before. Development suggested progress, which was itself a word the council did not hesitate to use. *Dei Verbum,* "On Divine Revelation," stated that the tradition of the church stemming from the apostles "makes progress in the church and grows" (*proficit et crescit,* n. 8). Tradition is not inert but dynamic.

Although the idea that tradition evolved won broad acceptance at the council, it was not without its problems, the most acute of which occurred in the debate on *Dignitatis Humanae,* "On Religious Liberty." Since the French Revolution, the popes had repeatedly condemned religious liberty and separation of church and state. But proponents of them at the council argued that they were legitimate developments of church teaching, an argument that to their opponents seemed like legerdemain. Development was supposedly movement to a further point along a given path, but *Dignitatis Humanae* seemed to jump off the given path to forge a new one.

Proponents of the change defended their position by making use of *ressourcement*. They maintained that popes in condemning separation of church and state were reacting against a specific historical situation that no longer prevailed. To discover how the church could now legitimately adapt to the new situation, it had to "return to the sources." In past tradition, it would find the fundamental truths that could guide it in the present situation. In this case, those truths were the church's consistent teaching that the act of faith had to be free and that for all individuals following their conscience was the ultimate moral norm.

Unlike development, a theory first straightforwardly proposed in the nineteenth century, *ressourcement* had enjoyed *avant la lettre* a truly venerable history in the Western church, beginning in the earliest centuries but emerging most notably with the Gregorian Reform of the eleventh century, the

campaign of popes and others to restore older canonical traditions. The reformers understood the
changes they fought to implement as a restoration
of the more authentic practice of an earlier era,
which implied a mandate to reinstate it.

Ressourcement was in its Latin form the motto of
the great humanists of the Renaissance—*Ad fontes!*
Return to the sources was, moreover, what moti-
vated the Protestant reformers as they sought to restore the authentic Gospel that in their opinion the
papal church had discarded and perverted. It lay
behind Pope Leo XIII's encyclical *Aeterni Patris,*
1879, initiating the revival of the study of Thomas
Aquinas. In fact, it lay behind virtually every reform
movement in the church and society in Western culture at least up to the Enlightenment.

In the mid-twentieth century, return to the
sources, now explicitly under the neologism *ressourcement,* drove much of the theological ferment
in France that played such a major role in Vatican
II. At the council virtually all the participants accepted the validity of the return-to-the-sources
principle. Disputes over it arose only when it seemed
to be applied too radically. Those who balked at such
application had a point because *ressourcement* had
more potent implications than development. While

development implies further movement along a given path, *ressourcement* says that we are no longer going to move along Path X. We are going back to a fork in the road and will now move along a better and different path.

Development and *ressourcement* are both about corporate memory, the memory that is constitutive of identity. What institutions wittingly or unwittingly chose to remember and chose to forget from their past makes them what they are. The great battles at Vatican II were battles over the identity of the church: not over its fundamental dogmas, but over the place, relevance, and respective weight of certain fundamental values in the tradition.

Vatican II did not solve the theoretical problem of how an institution by definition conservative handles the problem of change, nor was it the council's intention to do so. Councils are meetings that make decisions binding on the church. They are not meetings that solve theoretical problems, even though they must deal with the practical implications of such problems.

What is special about Vatican II in relationship to the two previous councils is, therefore, that it made its decisions with full awareness of the reality of change and full awareness that that reality affected the church in all its aspects. For a council to act with such an awareness of change is itself a significant change. Underlying the boldness with which the council accepted the reality of change was the assumption that appropriate change did not mean losing one's identity but, rather, enhancing it or salvaging it from ossification. If such change achieved its goal, it entailed a process of redefinition that was both continuous and discontinuous with the past.

3

Who Is in Charge?

FROM THE earliest centuries, the governance of the Christian church was both collegial and hierarchical. By the second century, bishops emerged as overseers and leaders of their respective communities and over the other ministers who served in them—deacons, presbyters, and, eventually, priests. As we have seen, in collegial fashion bishops called together their priests and others in councils / synods to deal with issues that had arisen in their domain. They sometimes joined in colleagueship with other bishops of the vicinity or province to deal with issues of wider import. A structure both collegial and hierarchical was in place.

No later than the third century, however, bishops were paying deference to the opinions of the bishop of Rome, and, once Christianity became the dominant religion in the Roman Empire, that deference became more pronounced, especially in the West. "Rome has spoken; the matter is settled," an expression taken from a sermon of Saint Augustine in the early fifth century, became a mantra for apologists for the doctrinal authority of the papacy. A new level of hierarchical structure had clearly emerged.

The four Gospels unambiguously testify to Peter as the leader of the twelve apostles, and credible sources indicate that Peter sometime after Jesus's resurrection traveled to Rome, where he was martyred. While in Rome, he, as one of the Twelve who had known and heard Jesus, surely acted as leader of the small and dispersed Christian communities in Rome at the time, and, therefore, acted in effect as bishop. This is the foundation for all later claims of popes to be the visible head of the Christian church.

Nonetheless, the churches continued to act as self-governing institutions under the leadership of their local bishops acting alone or in partnership with other bishops. In the second century, at least fifty councils took place in Palestine, North Africa, Rome, Gaul, and elsewhere. That number continued apace until the eventual disintegration of Roman institutions caused a diminishment, but councils /

synods never died out in the West even in the difficult centuries of the early medieval period. Although they generally dealt with problems related to the behavior of clerics, they sometimes made doctrinal decisions that became normative for the church at large. On both the local and the churchwide level, traditional church governance was synodal, that is, collegial.

When Constantine convoked the first churchwide council at Nicaea, he invited all the bishops of the empire. The bishop of Rome did not attend but sent two priests to represent him. The bishops at the council showed special respect to the Roman priests, but the priests played no notable role in the council's deliberations. In subsequent councils held in the Eastern Empire under imperial sponsorship, popes played roles ranging from important to marginal but never determinative.

The Great Schism with the Eastern church in 1054 occurred, not coincidentally, with the powerful resurgence of papal leadership claims in the Gregorian Reform. In the name of restoring a supposedly older and more authentic paradigm of church order, reformers in Rome created a new paradigm whose defining center was papal authority. The fierce resistance the Reform met testifies to its radical nature.

The Gregorian Reform raised in a newly explicit and confrontational way the crucial question of who in the church is empowered with final authority. The Reform asserted papal claims especially to counter imperial, regal, and ducal claims, and the popes often were able to count on bishops as their allies in the controversies that ensued.

Among the reformers, the most important, and the man for whom the movement was named, was Pope Gregory VII (r. 1073–1085). He is the reformer who made the most extreme claims for the authority of the pope, as codified in his document known as the *Dictatus Papae*, 1075, a set of propositions listing papal prerogatives as Gregory conceived them. Among them were, for instance, "That he may depose emperors," "That he himself may be judged by no one," and "That the pope is the only one whose feet are to be kissed by all princes." Although the *Dictatus* was not a public document and had no direct impact on events, it reveals a new and decisive assertion of papal claims to be in charge.

Even after the Gregorian Reform, popes, bishops, and secular rulers continued to recognize church-wide councils as the ultimate authority in the church. Nonetheless, popes now assumed the role as the only legitimate conveners of them, a role that became ever more widely accepted. Meanwhile, local and provincial councils met with regularity and, while acting in communion with the Holy See, made decisions binding on their locality virtually independently of it.

Despite the capacious claims for the papacy of the Gregorian Reformers, popes continued to look upon councils as the obvious and traditional instrument for addressing problems requiring serious attention, and they counted on bishops as partners in the enterprise. With the Council of Constance, 1414–1418, the smooth relationship between pope and council took a notable change for the worse.

Four decades earlier, in 1378, the Great Western Schism had broken out when two, then three men claimed to be the legitimate pope. The efforts of rulers and churchmen to end the schism availed nothing, as it dragged on for forty years. Finally, Emperor Sigismund prevailed upon one of the contenders to convoke a council at Constance to resolve the problem. Constance was successful in doing so but only by taking the drastic measure of deposing two of the contenders, persuading the third to resign, and proceeding to elect a new pope, Martin V.

Constance was not antipapal. It worked, in fact, to save the papacy. Nonetheless, from that point forward, popes became wary of councils. Matters took a further and more drastic turn for the worse with the Council of Basel, convoked by Pope Martin in 1431. As the result of an extraordinarily complex and contentious series of exchanges between the council and Martin's successor, Pope Eugene IV, the council deposed Eugene, elected a new pope, and unqualifiedly declared councils superior to popes. Eventually Eugene regained control of the situation through his convocation of another council at Florence, but the events threw into high relief the question of who had the last word in the church—the popes or the councils. Even if popes had the exclusive right to convoke a church-wide council, how much authority did a pope have over a council legitimately convoked? This question was only a specification of the larger question of the relationship of episcopal to papal authority. Not surprisingly, the question grabbed center stage at the Council of Trent, at Vatican Council I, and at Vatican Council II.

The Council of Trent

Shortly after Luther's excommunication in 1521, the cry arose, first in the Holy Roman Empire and then more widely, for a council to meet to deal with the doctrinal and reform issues he raised. The young Emperor Charles V soon emerged as the most insistent voice urging such a measure. Despite the immense pressure he applied to Pope Clement VII (r. 1523–1534), he met only evasion and deceptive promises. The specter of the radical measures taken by Constance and Basel haunted Clement and made him fearful that a council might act against him and his curia. Thus, even before the Council of Trent met, the question of its authority vis-à-vis the papacy's skulked in the background.

After Clement's death, the new pope, Paul III (r. 1534–1549), reversed his predecessor's policy and collaborated with Charles in efforts that finally led to the opening of the council at Trent on December 13, 1545. The council had hardly got under way when its relationship to the papacy unexpectedly arose. On January 4, 1546, the papal legates presiding at the council presented for approval a routine and innocuous document on "the manner of living," which exhorted everyone to prayer, fasting, courtesy in argument, and similarly uncontroversial behavior. They expected easy passage.

The document opened, "This holy synod lawfully assembled in the Holy Spirit . . ." The bishop of Fiesole, Braccio Martelli, intervened, insisting that the words "representing the universal church" be inserted after those opening words, in conformity, he said, with the practice of previous councils. The legates feared that that expression, which in fact only Constance and Basel had employed, might imply that the council had authority to act against the pope, and they sought therefore to prevent its insertion.

As the discussion evolved, the principal legate, Cardinal Giovanni Maria Del Monte, let slip that he would have to consult the pope on such a change. He thus unwittingly broached the question of the freedom, autonomy, and authority of the council and set off an explosion of verbal fireworks. Finally, arguments in favor of leaving the wording as it was prevailed, but the incident presaged a tension that for the rest of the council was never far from surfacing and that at times endangered the council's very viability.

The council lapsed into a suspension toward the end of the pontificate of Paul III. When in 1550 the new pope, Julius III, informed Charles V that he intended to reconvene it, he laid down a condition. The emperor had to assure him that the authority of the Holy See and the reform of the papal curia not be allowed on the agenda. Although those issues did not surface in a serious way during this second period of the council, 1551–1552, the fact that Julius felt it necessary to lay down his condition reveals how preoccupied the popes were with the turn a council might take. All three popes who convoked the three periods of the council—Paul III, Julius III, and Pius IV—strictly enjoined upon their legates to the council that they should under no circumstance allow the council to touch on the question of the authority of the Holy See or on the reform of the papal curia.

The great crisis at the council over papal authority arose only in the third and final period of the council, 1562–1563, under Pius IV, and it occurred once again over a seemingly unrelated issue. Among the most outrageous abuses prevalent in the church was the widespread absenteeism of bishops from their dioceses and pastors from their parishes. That is, bishops and pastors collected the benefice attached to their office and then used part of the money to hire vicars to do the job for them. Even more outrageous were the prelates who held several bishoprics at once, resided in only one or in none of them, and collected the money from them all. Luther's *bête noire,* Cardinal Albert of Brandenburg, held three such benefices, as he was simultaneously archbishop of Mainz and of Magdeburg and administrator of the diocese of Halberstadt.

All previous attempts to correct such abuses had failed because popes, in exchange for a financial consideration, had dispensed petitioners from the canons that required residence and that forbade the simultaneous holding of incompatible benefices. Reformers at the council became convinced, therefore, that the only way to uproot the problem lay in finding a way to obviate such dispensations. They determined to close that loophole, a measure that directly implicated papal authority.

The way to close the loophole was to declare that residence was not simply a canonical regulation but a law of God, *jus divinum*. Popes might have expansive authority, but they certainly could not dispense from God's law. By the spring of 1562, reformers proposed this solution and thereby divided the council into two factions, each holding passionately to its position. The first, which favored *jus divinum,* comprised virtually all the non-Italian bishops but also included a number of Italians. The second, almost exclusively Italian, argued that *jus divinum* was contrary to the practice of the church, which had consistently allowed dispensation, that it would impede the proper functioning of the papal curia, and that it infringed upon papal authority. That last argument was, obviously, the most serious and the most likely to end in an ugly confrontation. It raised the forbidden issue.

The confrontation indeed occurred and lasted for a full ten months between the middle of September 1562 and the middle of July the next year. During that long period, the council suffered a bitter crisis that prevented it from passing a single piece of legislation. The council was at a standstill. Girolamo Seripando, one of the papal legates, wrote to Rome, "No letter can convey to you how difficult things really are here."

Not until July was Cardinal Giovanni Morone, the leading papal legate, able to work out a formula to which both parties assented. The decree avoided saying explicitly that residence was a divine law, but insisted, rather, that by divine ordinance bishops had to preach to their flocks and perform other sacred duties, which they obviously could not do if they were absent. Morone's solution did not fully satisfy either party, but it was the best that could be done. From the great crisis at Trent, therefore, no clear answer emerged as to who was in charge.

Vatican I

Although no clear answer emerged, the Council of Trent was quintessentially a bishop-centered council. From beginning to end, the council strove to enhance the dignity and uphold the authority of the local bishop. The effort to do so generally took the form of imposing reforms on the episcopacy with the goal of restoring to it its traditional rights and duties. The obligation to hold synods at regular intervals, for instance, was among the rights and duties the council reinforced.

During the council, many leading Catholics, including many bishops present at Trent, blamed the popes for its travails, and they had good reason for doing so, especially for trying to keep reform of the curia off the agenda. Once the council finally came to a successful conclusion, however, critics were ready to forget their grievances against the popes and work with them in common cause. Popes themselves enacted reform measures that won approval, even though those measures did not go far enough to satisfy the more exacting critics. They projected a new image of themselves as dutiful and devout pastors. In Rome, they engaged in intelligent city planning and enhanced the city with beautiful monuments to establish Rome as the cultural capital of Europe. Within a few decades of the closing of Trent, papal prestige was higher than it had been for a long time.

It eventually began to decline. By the middle of the eighteenth century, the decline was dramatic. The causes, multiple and too complex for treatment here, were in general the result of the convergence of ideologies such as Gallicanism, Jansenism, and a burgeoning nationalism allied with anti-clerical and rationalist strains of the continental Enlightenment. In the political and ecclesiastical philosophy represented by this coalition, the pope enjoyed respect but only the degree of authority his flock might concede to him, which often was very little. The French Revolution and its Pan-European aftermath carried these traditions with them and led to the captivity and death in France of Pope Pius VI in 1799. With that event, the end of the papacy, so often predicted, had now finally arrived.

Or so it seemed. A reaction to the Revolution and to the philosophies that underlay it was inevitable. Liberty, equality, and fraternity had resulted in political chaos and the destruction, physical and psychological, of much that people held dear. The toll the triad had taken on the church was immense. Churches were sacked, monasteries destroyed, and priests, nuns, and bishops sent to the guillotine without cause.

During the Napoleonic era, Pope Pius VII, successor to the unfortunate Pius VI, emerged as one of the few leaders who stood up to Napoleon. He had held his ground in negotiating with him the Concordat of 1801 that allowed the church once again to function publicly in France. He had, moreover, eventually excommunicated Napoleon. Pius paid a heavy price for it, which included arrest and exile. But he survived with his head still on and held high. Papal prestige began to rise again.

This context gave birth to the powerful grassroots movement known as Ultramontanism. The word "ultramontane" originated in Italy in the Middle Ages to denote a pope from northern Europe *(papa ultramontano),* that is, "from the other side of the mountain," the Alps. In the early modern period, the Germans and the French reversed its meaning to refer to the southern side of the Alps, that is, Rome, and therefore to people who supported papal authority over regal or episcopal authority.

The word as well as the reality caught on. For the ultramontanes, the papacy stood as a source of stability in the political and social chaos that seemed ever threatening. Thoroughgoing ultramontanes saw papal authority in terms that defy exaggeration and that seemed not simply to downgrade but to abolish episcopal and synodal authority. To a virtually absolute version of papal primacy, they attached a similarly absolute version of papal infallibility. Even for the less zealous ultramontanes, there was no question as to who was in charge.

Even if much of the impetus for the movement came from the belief that a powerful and infallible papacy provided the only feasible antidote to the aberrations of the modern world, an uncritical and newly benign interpretation of the role the papacy played in society in the Middle Ages was also important. The Romantic movement supplied the lens and the vocabulary to make this interpretation attractive and seem reasonable.

Although the ultramontane campaign began in France, it soon had counterparts elsewhere on the continent. Laymen played a large role in promoting it, and they did so largely through the popular press. Particularly important in this regard was Louis Veuillot, editor of the Parisian journal *L'Univers,* which by the middle of the century waged an aggressive, no-holds-barred campaign in favor of an extreme form of papal centralization and against those he perceived as enemies of the ultramontane movement.

Veuillot aimed his campaign especially against French bishops who held opinions less pope-centered than his own.

The opponents to Veuillot and to the movement were known as gallicans, but they were a pale shadow of the gallicans of the seventeenth and eighteenth centuries. Like their predecessors, they advocated an episcopacy with strong prerogatives, especially when gathered in synod. They held fast to the traditional belief that ecumenical councils were the highest authority in the church. As post-Revolution Catholics, however, they supported a degree of papal authority in the church greater than did many of the gallicans who had gone before them. But they saw the papacy as the center where everything came together rather than, as did the ultramontanes, the center from which everything flowed. The difference between them and the more moderate ultramontanes, however, was often more a matter of label than substance.

Pius IX was the pope who presided over the ultramontane-gallican controversy. Although he at first seemed to stand above it, he very shortly threw his support to the ultramontanes, and it grew ever more ardent and unqualified. Nonetheless, when in the mid-1860s he began considering the possibility of convoking a council, he saw it most immediately as an antidote to the "evils of the times" rather than as an instrument to vindicate papal authority. In his mind, however, the two aims became almost indistinguishable.

By the time the council opened on December 8, 1869, the controversy over the meaning of primacy and infallibility had reached such a pitch that the council could not possibly avoid dealing with it. Vatican I was unevenly divided between the two parties. The gallicans could claim at most only 20 percent of the membership. Among that number, however, were holders of some of the most important sees in Europe—Paris, Mainz, Munich, Vienna, Prague, Turin, and Milan. Also among them were the archbishops of Saint Louis and Cincinnati, two of the most important sees in the United States at that time.

Once *Pastor Aeternus* was introduced to the council, it excited controversy, not so much over the three chapters on primacy but over the fourth, on infallibility. The bishops of the minority believed strongly in papal preeminence in teaching and even subscribed to papal infallibility. They objected, however, to the wording of the document on three counts. According to them, it allowed interpretations of infallibility as (1) absolute or unqualified, (2) personal, a quality of the pope's person rather than an aspect of his office, and (3) separate, as if the pope could act independently of the church, even in opposition to a council. In that last regard, they argued that *Pastor Aeternus* proposed a version of infallibility that severed the head of the church from the body.

In the end, the bishops failed to reach a consensus. On July 17, 1870, the day before the final vote on *Pastor Aeternus,* sixty opponents to the decree decided to depart for home that evening rather than cast a negative ballot. The next day 535 bishops assembled in Saint Peter's, a number down about 25 percent from the opening day. The notably smaller number was a sad and potentially ominous note amid the jubilation over the passage of the decree by the bishops present with only two dissenting votes.

With *Pastor Aeternus,* the council seemed to have decided with finality who was in charge. Moreover, if the bishops who absented themselves because of it were correct in their interpretation, it had done so to such a decree that it invested all authority in the papacy and thereby rendered councils superfluous. Vatican I was the council that put an end to councils and that thereby abolished the collegial tradition in church governance.

Vatican II

Catholicism is, however, too complex, too capacious, too lumbering, and too rich in traditions to function in the absolutist and unqualifiedly top-down mode that the extreme ultramontanes attributed to *Pastor Aeternus.* Those features of Catholicism imbue the church with a self-qualifying and self-correcting potential, which began to manifest itself right after the council. The Roman Congregations, for instance, began to accept interpretations of the decree that allowed its opponents finally to give their assent. Crucial in this regard, of course, was the stance of the pope himself.

During the council, the intervention on June 18, 1870, by Cardinal Filippo Maria Guidi had provided a moment when the gallicans and the moderate ultramontanes achieved accord. Guidi directly addressed two of the gallicans' objections to the wording of the decree. He explained that infallibility pertained not to the person of the pope but to his office and that the pope was independent of the church only in the sense that councils did not confer infallibility upon him. The pope was required, however, to learn from bishops what the sense of the church was on an issue in question.

Pope Pius IX in a stormy interview with Guidi after his speech utterly rejected Guidi's interpretation with his famous outburst, "I am the church. I am tradition." These were claims that implied that infallibility was a quality of his person and that the pope could act independently of the church. Yet, after the council circumstances led him to express himself less absolutely and to ease the way to more moderate interpretations. Especially important in that regard was the necessity he felt to side with the German bishops in their defense of *Pastor Aeternus* against the extreme interpretation of it by Chancellor Bismarck.

When almost a half-century later, in 1918, the first Code of Canon Law appeared, it contained two canons that manifested the ambiguity that remained even many decades after Vatican l. Canon 228 stated categorically: "An ecumenical council enjoys supreme authority over the universal church." Canon 222, however, stated that the Roman Pontiff alone has the right to convoke a council. It continued: "It is the right of the Roman Pontiff to preside over an ecumenical council either in person or through delegates. It is his right to determine and designate the subjects to be treated and the order for doing so. It is his right to transfer, suspend, and dissolve a council and to confirm its decrees."

Whatever the theoretical answer to the question of who was in charge, in the decades immediately following the council, the popes began to assume a decree of practical authority in the church more unquestioned and more comprehensive than had their predecessors. They did so partly as a consequence of *Pastor Aeternus* and partly as a consequence of changes in society at large, such as the greater centralization of authority taking place in most institutions of any size. Local councils did not altogether disappear, but their number greatly diminished, as did the importance and authority attributed to them. Bishops sometimes complained (in private) that they had become little more than delivery boys for decisions of the Roman curia. The center seemed to enjoy absolute control.

In this context, Pope John XXIII's announcement on January 25, 1959, that he intended to convoke a council came as a shock. It with one blow sent chasing the common belief that *Pastor Aeternus* had spelled the end of ecumenical councils, and it thereby suggested that, after all, bishops still enjoyed a crucial role in the governance of the universal church. The very event of Vatican II is, therefore, the best interpretation of *Pastor Aeternus.*

In the three and a half years of preparation that elapsed before the council finally opened, a consensus arose that the new council should examine aspects of the church that under the pressure of time Vatican I had not been able to do. Among those aspects was the office of bishops in the church. By the time Vatican II opened, many participants were resolved to make sure that the role of bishops and of the local church received proper attention. Scholars had, moreover, laid the foundation for the resolve by their less ultramontane histories of church governance.

The issue entered the stage of the council in the very first document the council addressed, *Sacrosanctum Concilium,* "On the Sacred Liturgy." Ever since the establishment of the Congregation of Rites by Pope Sixtus V in the late sixteenth century, the Congregation had assumed exclusive oversight of the liturgy. *Sacrosanctum* specified, however, that "the regulation of the liturgy within certain limits belongs also to various kinds of groups of bishops legitimately established with competence in given territories" (n. 22). Though some bishops strenuously objected to this provision, it passed easily.

In strongest terms, *Sacrosanctum* insisted that the full participation of the congregation was essential for genuine liturgy. *Lex orandi, lex credendi,* that is, the mode of prayer is the mode of the church (nn. 14–20). As already mentioned, the definition of the church as "the people of God," the burden of the second chapter of *Lumen Gentium,* also pointed to the collegial mode of the church. The very word "dialogue," so frequently invoked by the council, sometimes stands almost as code for that mode. Thus, a careful reading of the documents of the council reveals that, sometimes obviously and sometimes subtly, the collegial constitution of the church became a pervasive theme at Vatican II.

The third chapter of *Lumen Gentium* is entitled "On the Hierarchical Constitution of the Church." It is, however, just as much about the collegial constitution of the church as the hierarchical. It explicitly teaches that the relationship between the pope and the bishops, especially bishops gathered in council, is collegial. In so teaching, it was simply putting a word to what was actually happening, imperfectly and sometimes uncomfortably, in the very way Vatican II was functioning.

At the moment the teaching was proposed, however, it set off a difficult confrontation between the overwhelming majority of the bishops, who favored the proposal, and a minority adamantly opposed to it. The minority argued that episcopal collegiality was incompatible with *Pastor Aeternus.*

Despite the objections of the minority, the council moved ahead "to profess before all and to declare the teaching that bishops, successors of the apostles, together with Peter's successor, the Vicar of Christ and the visible head of the whole church, govern the house of the living God" (n. 18). The teaching was clear. At an ecumenical council, collegiality was the mode in which a council functioned. But if even in that situation problems arose about how collegiality was to function, how it was to function outside a council was even more problematic. What was the appropriate instrument or institution to make collegiality an ongoing reality in the church?

In September 1965, on the day the fourth and final period of the council opened, Pope Paul VI issued a *motu proprio* ("on his own initiative") establishing the Synod of Bishops. The council subsequently accepted the Synod of Bishops as the mode of making collegiality operative. As a careful examination of the document reveals, however, the Synod of Bishops is an instrument of papal primacy.

Who is in charge? The council answered the question by reaffirming the ancient tradition that church governance is both hierarchical and collegial. It reaffirmed the primacy of the pope and the collective authority of the bishops. It thus gave the traditional and authentic answer, but it was an answer whose practical implementation will by definition always be untidy. Church governance, like the governance of every institution that is not a dictatorship, consists of lines that are sometimes blurred.

The question facing the Catholic church today, therefore, is not the theoretical question of who is in charge. Vatican Council II answered that question. The question today is the question Vatican II did not have the opportunity to answer: What are the appropriate instruments for making the collegial (synodal) tradition of church governance practical and effective? Working out the answers to the question will not always be neat and clear, but such is the condition of real life. In any case, the instruments, while genuinely collegial, must at the same time firmly uphold the primacy of the Roman Pontiff. Only thus will they conform to the ancient collegial and hierarchical tradition of the church.

PART TWO

Participants

4

Popes and Curia

COUNCILS are meetings of bishops. Others may participate, but bishops constitute the essential membership. This is not simply an ecclesiastical ordinance but a consistent historical phenomenon from the earliest local councils up to and including Vatican II. Over the course of the centuries, however, the percentage of the church-wide episcopacy that participated in ecumenical councils has varied considerably.

The divergence in percentage holds for the three councils we are considering. The Council of Trent opened with only twenty-nine bishops, roughly 5 percent of the total episcopacy. At its peak, it numbered only slightly over 200, out of an episcopacy of well over 600. At Vatican I, the approximately 700 bishops who opened the council came from a worldwide episcopacy of about 1,050. However, departures during the council, including those who left the day before the final vote on *Pastor Aeternus,* brought the number down to 530 on that last day. Some 2,400 bishops attended the first period of Vatican II, accounting for around 90 percent of the episcopacy. Ill health, difficulty in travel, and obstruction by governments were common reasons for failure to participate.

In the wake of the Gregorian Reform, a new category of ecclesiastical dignity arose known as cardinals, bishops from towns near Rome such as Ostia and Palestrina on whom a decree of Pope Nicholas II in 1059 confided the right to elect the pope. Pope Nicholas's decree had massive repercussions. It raised these formerly marginal ecclesiastics to what in time became one of the most powerful positions in the church.

Soon the number of cardinals was increased by the addition of deacons and priests, who also had the right to participate in papal elections. (Only on the eve of Vatican II did Pope John XXIII decree that cardinals be bishops.) Most cardinals resided in or near Rome and played an ever more determining role in the day-to-day business of the papal curia. Their role in the three councils varied.

None of the three popes who convoked the three periods of the Council of Trent ever set foot in the council. They were present vicariously through cardinal legates, who presided over the council in their name. At Vatican I and Vatican II, the popes presided in person at the relatively few solemn public sessions but absented themselves from the working sessions. As at Trent, they appointed the cardinals who chaired the working sessions. Through them and through other means, they kept themselves well informed about what was going on in the basilica, a task that closed-circuit television made easier for John XXIII and Paul VI.

The Council of Trent

For the Council of Trent, the distance of the popes from the assembly was more than metaphorical. Trent was hundreds of miles from Rome. Pope Paul III excused himself from traveling there because of old age. Pope Pius IV (r. 1559–1565), under pressure from Emperor Ferdinand I to appear before the council to resolve the great crisis in 1563, excused himself because of poor health, but fear of how the assembly might react to his presence surely played a part in his decision.

The legates the popes appointed to preside in their stead were cardinal bishops drawn from the curia. At the first period of Trent, there were, after the first few months, two, at the second period one, and at the third period generally four. Aside from them, no other cardinals from the curia participated in the council. The body of curial cardinals remained in Rome. There they were able to influence the council indirectly by influencing the popes, who felt themselves bound to consult them regularly as a body gathered for that purpose,

In comparison with the roles the cardinals of the curia played in Vatican I and Vatican II, their role at the Council of Trent was marginal. The role of the cardinal legates at Trent was, however, crucial. They received precise and sometimes peremptory instructions from Rome as to what they were to allow the assembly to treat, as well as on other subjects related to the ongoing business of the council. The legates, kept on a short leash by the popes, did not have an easy task. They had to deal with an assembly jealous of its authority and with pressure from secular rulers, for whom the decisions of the council had potentially serious repercussions in their realms. Although the legates were the popes' men, they found themselves having also to serve two other masters.

The popes themselves were far from having a free hand. If Pope Paul III had prevailed when he first convoked the council, he would have limited the agenda to doctrinal issues and reserved to himself the reform of the church. Emperor Charles V took precisely the opposite position. When the assembly voted to treat both issues, Paul had to yield. In the last period of the council, Pope Pius IV, despite his earlier insistence that reform of the papal curia was absolutely off limits for the council, finally had to agree to it in at least a few particulars.

The bishops chafed under what they considered illegitimate papal interference in the free functioning of the council. Besides the tight control his legates tried to exercise, Pope Pius IV at one point threatened to send to Trent more bishops from the Papal States who would vote according to his wishes. Under such circumstances, it is no wonder that during and after the council critics questioned whether the council was free and therefore whether it was legitimate.

The classic work in that regard is the *Istoria del Concilio Tridentino*, 1619, by the Venetian priest Paolo Sarpi, a member of the Servite Order. Sarpi argued that the council was a tragic story of the failure of true reform and of the triumph of papal

PARTICIPANTS

abuse of power. Although immediately put on the papal Index of Forbidden Books, Sarpi's book was translated into the major European languages, sometimes in multiple editions. Not until the twentieth century did the German historian Hubert Jedin produce an academically sound history of the council that put Sarpi's claims into perspective.

Vatican I

The first step for understanding Vatican I is that it met in the Vatican. Five earlier councils had met in Rome, at the site of the popes' cathedral of Saint John Lateran. Vatican I was, therefore, not special for meeting in Rome, but it was special for meeting in Rome at a certain time in history. Pius, seemingly without second thought, chose the site. Bishops and others seemingly accepted it almost as a foregone conclusion. In contrast, the painful and protracted negotiations in the sixteenth century about where to hold what became the Council of Trent assumed that Rome was utterly out of the question as an appropriate site.

Had a pope even of the seventeenth or eighteenth century decided to convoke a council in Rome, he would have met with considerable opposition. By the third quarter of the nineteenth century, however, the ultramontane movement had reached a crescendo. Even bishops opposed to the movement were ultramontane enough to accept that the council take place "on the other side of the mountain," that is, in Rome. Not for centuries had the papacy enjoyed such solid and practical support from the episcopacy.

The support extended to the pope's curia. This situation allowed Pius to proceed with the arrangements for the council without fear of serious challenge. It allowed him to appoint curial cardinals to preside at the council. In that regard, he of course had the precedent of Trent to justify his actions. But his support also allowed him to employ the curia in planning the council and in preparing the documents for it. For that, he did not have a precedent from Trent. By meeting in the Vatican, the council met in the institution where, under the pope, the curia was in charge. Nothing could be more natural or more efficient than for the curia to provide services to help the council along its way.

In early 1865, Pius appointed five curia cardinals to a Central Commission to direct preparations for the council. At its first meeting, the Central Commission recommended that the materials for discussion at the council be prepared in Rome beforehand.

Preparing the documents means preparing the agenda. Preparing the agenda means having considerable control over the direction the council might take. The contrast with Trent is stark. For better or for worse, Trent opened without a single document prepared for it.

As preparation of the council by the curia became known, it provoked concern and even resentment. That provision, plus the secrecy that enveloped the preparations, gave rise to rumors and sometimes almost paranoid fears about what was being planned. Prime ministers of European states were prominent among those who, even before the council opened, expressed concern over what it might attempt. But such fears and concerns were not strong enough or widespread enough to have any practical impact.

By the time of Vatican I, the curia had a departmental structure that it lacked at the time of the Council of Trent. A few decades after Trent, Pope Sixtus V (r. 1585–1590) organized the curia into departments called congregations, each with a specific area of oversight and each headed by a cardinal, the same structure that is in place today. The Congregation of the Holy Office of the Roman Inquisition, for instance, oversaw doctrine, and the Congregation of Rites oversaw worship.

At its second meeting, March 10, 1865, the Central Commission recommended the creation of further commissions to apportion the preparatory work. It also recommended that these commissions be extensions of the corresponding congregations of the curia and that they draw their members principally from the personnel of those congregations. That personnel, the Central Commission argued, had the large perspective needed for an ecumenical council because it had to deal on almost a daily basis with issues facing the church worldwide. Moreover, the congregations of the curia were "the guardians of the traditions of the Holy See." Pius IX accepted the recommendation.

He meanwhile consulted in great secrecy a small number of bishops about what issues the council needed to deal with. He received many suggestions, most of which related to church discipline. There was a general consensus, however, that the rationalism and religious skepticism of "the modern world" had to be at the top of the agenda. Despite the momentum the ultramontane movement had gathered by this time, only relatively few bishops mentioned infallibility as an issue to be dealt with.

Pius saw to it that recommendations were communicated to the appropriate preparatory commissions. In formulating the documents for the council, the commissions made faithful and fair use of the recommendations. They thus showed themselves ready to follow the direction the council might take and not try to force it to follow some predetermined direction of their own.

Pius determined that as soon as the council opened, the bishops would elect twenty-four members to each of the four deputations charged with revising the draft documents in the light of the discussion in Saint Peter's, but he also appointed a curia cardinal to head each of the deputations.

The five cardinals who presided at the working sessions did so fairly and evenhandedly. Cardinal Luigi Bilio, who headed the doctrinal deputation, the only one of the four deputations whose documents the council dealt with, showed himself similarly evenhanded, sometimes to the displeasure of the pope. As the council actually functioned, therefore, the major role the curia played did not inhibit the free flow of discussion in the basilica, nor, despite the suspicions that surrounded the preparations, did the bishops complain or have grounds to complain that the curia was trying to control the council.

There is no reason to believe that consciously or unconsciously Pius saw his use of the curia cardinals in the preparation of the council and as its officers once it had begun as a way to secure greater control over the council. Nor did he in fact secure more control by the key positions he accorded them. Nonetheless, the key positions those cardinals held highlight the strongly papal character of Vatican I even apart from the actions of the pope himself in relation to the bishops gathered in the basilica. If Trent was quintessentially bishop-centered, Vatican I was quintessentially pope-centered. It was pope-centered (and curia-centered) even apart from *Pastor Aeternus.*

The behavior of Pius IX made the council even more pope-centered. Although not physically present in the basilica, the pope was virtually present with a force and direct impact denied the popes of the Council of Trent. Once infallibility reached the floor of the council, he abandoned his earlier protestations of neutrality on the question and became an open partisan. By word and deed, he communicated his position to the assembly and gave heart to advocates of the most extreme interpretation of the doctrine. His confrontation with Cardinal Guidi, for instance, took place in his apartments, but reports of it reached the bishops almost immediately and destroyed the hope raised by Guidi's intervention that a meeting of minds between the moderates of both parties might happen.

The physical proximity of the pope to the assembly in Saint Peter's had another important impact on the council's workings. In theory, the council had the mechanism it needed to conduct its business without recourse to the pope to resolve procedural matters. But Pius's proximity proved too great a temptation to both parties in the council. Each of them ran to him to intervene in their favor. Although Pius at times referred matters back to the council, he gave willing ear to the infallibility party and lent it his prestige.

Vatican II

Four months after Pope John announced his intention of convoking a council, he named the members of the so-called Ante-Preparatory Commission that was to gather the information to be used in the actual preparation of the council. The commission worked under the leadership of Cardinal Domenico Tardini, John's secretary of state.

Tardini asked the bishops of the world and the Catholic universities to submit issues they deemed in need of action. When by the spring of 1960 the commission had organized the immense amount of material that arrived, Pope John formally closed this ante-preparatory stage. He then established ten preparatory commissions, whose task was to create draft documents for submission to the council. As heads of these commissions, he named the prefects (or secretaries) of the curia congregations according to the issues in question. For example, Cardinal Alfredo Ottaviani, secretary of the Holy Office, headed the preparatory Theological Commission. As the date for the opening of the council approached, the pope designated the same cardinals to head the corresponding ten commissions of the council itself.

In making these appointments, John XXIII followed the precedent set by Vatican I. Even before the council opened, however, criticism mounted from bishops and others that the preparatory commissions rigidly excluded viewpoints that the cardinals in charge did not share. The criticism singled out the Theological Commission as the chief offender in this regard. It was a harbinger of the conflict that erupted a month after the council opened when the council rejected *De Fontibus,* "On the Sources of Revelation," the draft document submitted to it by Cardinal Ottaviani's Theological Commission (now called the Doctrinal Commission). The council found the document out of touch with current scholarship and, among other things, too negative in its approach. Thus began a tug-of-war between the majority of the assembly in Saint Peter's and the commissions responsible for the documents. The war continued until under the impact of new members the commissions finally became more responsive to the assembly's wishes.

Unlike Vatican I, therefore, the controlling positions the curia cardinals enjoyed elicited resentment and sharp criticism. "The curia" became for the majority at the council the mantra that expressed the persistent suspicion that a small group of highly placed prelates were ready to use almost any means to frustrate the direction the council was taking. Although in the curia there were many who generally supported the majority, the suspicion was all too often substantiated.

Like Pius IX, Pope John XXIII appeared in Saint Peter's during the council only for the solemn public ceremonies, but, as mentioned, he was able in his apartment to follow what transpired in the basilica. He maintained a hands-off policy regarding the developments on the floor of the council.

On November 21, 1962, however, he intervened to resolve a procedural stalemate that occurred over the vote on "On the Sources of Revelation." The previous day the council had voted overwhelmingly to reject the document, but the vote fell slightly short of the two-thirds required for a rejection. The result would force the council to continue to debate a document that most of the bishops found fundamentally flawed.

John sent word to Saint Peter's that although the vote did not fully satisfy the technicality of the council's procedures, it indicated that continuing discussion might not be the way to reconcile the various opinions that had surfaced on the matter. Therefore, "yielding to the wishes of many," he decided to refer the document to a "mixed commission," made up of members of the Doctrinal Commission, the original author, and members of the Secretariat for Promoting Christian Unity.

John had created the Secretariat before the council and eventually gave it a status equivalent to that of the ten formal commissions. He appointed as its head Cardinal Augustin Bea, former rector of the Pontifical Biblical Institute in Rome, who was not a member of the curia. During the debate on "On the Sources of Revelation," Bea and members of the Secretariat had mounted the severest criticism of the document.

John's intervention was strictly procedural. It did not touch on the substance of the matter under discussion. It marked, however, a great turning point in the council. In the first place, it gave encouragement to those critical of the documents prepared for them under the auspices of the curia. In the second, by giving the Secretariat equal status in reformulating the document, it directly qualified the authority of the Doctrinal Commission, which claimed supervisory authority over all the documents of the council. To some at the council the Doctrinal Commission at times seemed to claim supervisory authority over the council itself.

At the end of the council's first period, John made another crucial intervention by establishing a Coordinating Commission with almost plenipotentiary authority to oversee the revision of the preparatory documents. Of the eight cardinals of the commission, only two were from the curia. John thereby weakened the dominant, even dominating, role certain members of the curia had until that point assumed.

Pope John died on June 3, 1963. Paul VI succeeded him. The new pope was slow to judge and keen on pondering both sides of a question. He felt his responsibilities heavily, sometimes giving the impression that the whole burden of the church fell on his shoulders. His personality and his background prompted him, therefore, to intervene frequently in the council, which he did in matters great and small. He sent the commissions his "recommendations" or sometimes his blunt orders for the improvement of their texts. The popes during Trent had scarce opportunity for such interventions. Pius IX did so only once, and John XXIII, as we have seen, confined his interventions to procedural questions.

Paul's interventions had the unfortunate consequence of undermining the regular procedures of the council and of encouraging the idea that bishops could call upon the pope to reverse decisions with which they disagreed. Paul often found himself besieged. When he felt his authority challenged, he could be stubborn, which further complicated the situation.

The root of the problem, however, was not the personality of the pope but the ambiguity of the pope's relationship to the council. The regulations *(Ordo Concilii)* governing the council's procedures assumed, in accordance with canon 222 of the Code of Canon Law, that the pope had ultimate authority regarding the council, but they failed to indicate in any detail just how that authority functioned. Could the pope do whatever he wanted? If so, why bother with a council at all?

Once Paul VI became pope, this problem took concrete form. Paul sometimes seemed to want his "recommendations" to be considered on the same level as those of any other bishop at the council, but more often he took a proactive role and expected acquiescence to his interventions, which were many. He sometimes under pressure reversed a decision he had earlier made. At other times, he seemed to act as interpreter to the council of its meaning, sometimes as a monitor of its orthodoxy, and sometimes as a rival to its authority. The multiplicity of roles Paul played led to confusion on the part of the bishops and sometimes to resentment.

The failure of the council's procedures to spell out who on the council floor was responsible for what exacerbated the situation. But the ultimate cause was the complexity of the relationship between bishops and popes. Vatican Council II determined that the relationship was both hierarchical and collegial, but, as we have seen, it did not determine how even in a council the relationship between the two was to function.

5

Theologians

Only with the founding of universities in the thirteenth century did theologians emerge as a category of teachers clearly distinct from bishops. Until that time, bishops had the task, shared in a limited way with pastors, of instructing their flocks in the basic truths of the faith and of engaging in controversy to settle contemporary issues. Their formal education was fundamentally the same as that of other members of the upper classes of society and was based mainly on the literary classics of ancient Greece and Rome. If all went well, however, they at a certain point began to study the Bible and other sacred texts.

Saint Augustine, a teacher of rhetoric before his conversion, stands as a paradigm for this tradition of bishop-teachers. Sometimes abbots, mitered churchmen that they were, also became renowned teachers of the faith. In that regard, Saint Bernard is outstanding, but with the "new learning" of the universities looming on the horizon in his day, he marked the end of the era of the nonprofessional theologian.

By the early decades of the thirteenth century, the universities were on their way to becoming one of the most important and characteristic institutions of society, even though they trained only a miniscule percentage of the population. They had already developed highly sophisticated programs for training professionals in law, medicine, and theology. They certified the professional competence of those who completed their programs by conferring official approval in the form of degrees such as master and doctor.

The doctoral program in theology at universities such as Paris was too long and too rigorous to appeal to many young men who hoped to advance to the episcopal dignity. It most characteristically produced, therefore, not future bishops but future teachers of theology in the same pattern as the teachers who had taught them. It was a self-reproducing system. This was particularly true for those intrepid individuals who persevered through a dozen years of advanced schooling to win the doctoral crown. In some universities that had doctoral programs in theology, the programs were shorter and less exacting than at Paris. Truly ambitious students, however, wanted a program like that of Paris that held to the highest standards of the profession.

The result was an episcopacy in which a relative few held advanced theological degrees, in which a few more might hold a degree in canon law, in which a larger number might boast of a smattering of university schooling, and in which a still larger number was virtually innocent of university-style learning. This did not mean the bishops were ignorant men, but it did mean they lacked the skills to deal with the ever more technical questions and problems that arose in an ever more sophisticated society. Many of those questions and problems resulted, in fact, from disagreements among the professional theologians themselves.

The further result was the emergence of theologians "of the schools," which meant teachers trained in the universities. These theologians spent their days analyzing and debating issues that earlier generations had glossed over. Their learning became ever more technical, which led to the development of a technical vocabulary unintelligible to those not initiated into it.

This was an entirely new situation. It produced for the church two classes of teachers—bishops, who had the right to teach because they were successors of the apostles, and theologians, who claimed the right to teach by virtue of their professional training. The situation produced a bifurcation that sometimes resulted in fruitful collaboration but at other times in resentment and rivalry.

Powerful theological faculties such as those of the University of Paris and the University of Cologne did not hesitate to pronounce condemnations of peers who deviated from the faith. While the bishops remained silent, the theological faculty of the University of Louvain condemned Luther, and it did so in November 1519, months before the papal bull of Luther's excommunication was ready and in circulation. By the sixteenth century, the public ecclesiastical role of faculties of theology was considerable and unchallenged.

The forum in which the two classes of teachers officially and most fruitfully collaborated was the general councils. The collaboration began early. In 1274, for instance, Saint Thomas Aquinas died on his way to the Second Council of Lyons. By the mid-fifteenth century, theologians even enjoyed voting rights virtually equivalent to those of the bishops, but the practice was soon suppressed. Theologians became essentially a resource that the bishops used as seemed expedient to them.

Lateran Council V (1512–1517), the council that preceded Trent, made minimal use of theologians. Although Pope Julius II (r. 1503–1513) urged them to come to the council, he excluded them from any active role and limited them to simple witnesses to the council's deliberations, on the same level with the knights and curial officials who were present. The theologians' fortunes improved in the next three councils.

The Council of Trent

After eleven years of frustrating attempts to convene a council, impeded by wars and political machinations, Pope Paul III finally succeeded in doing so. As it became apparent that the council was actually going to happen, he appointed the three cardinal-legates to preside at the council in his name. Despite the time that elapsed between their appointment and the opening of the council, the legates undertook virtually no preparation of either the agenda or the procedures. In both those regards, the council under the leadership of the legates had to determine on its own how to proceed. The role the theologians played at Trent evolved, therefore, in pragmatic fashion as needs arose.

The legates laid down no conditions for admission of theologians and seemed to assume that rulers would choose and send them. In any case, that is what happened. Pope Paul III sent two, whose only privilege was to speak first whenever the legates summoned the theologians to express their opinions on a given issue. In contrast, Francis I, the king of France, sent twelve. The emperor sent fewer than Francis but more than did the pope. King John III of Portugal sent fewer still. In addition, a few bishops brought theologians with them as advisers. By February 1546, just two months after the council opened, twenty-seven theologians had already arrived. It seems that only one, a chaplain to Cardinal Pole, was from the secular clergy. The others were members of religious orders, which had well-established provisions for the theological training of their members.

The theologians generally came from prestigious universities, such as Paris, Coimbra, and Louvain, and they took their responsibilities seriously. The superiors general of the religious orders surely saw to it that their theologians at the council were men of distinguished achievement. Throughout the long years of the council, the caliber of the theologians was high.

Not chosen by a central authority, the theologians therefore did not represent a unified viewpoint except that they had not embraced Lutheranism. As the acts of the council show, they felt perfectly free to express their opinion on a given issue, whatever that opinion might be. The popes were not keen on the theologians from the University of Paris because of their conciliarist sympathies, but they made no attempt to bar them from the council.

When the first theologians arrived at Trent, they received no instructions about their responsibilities. The bishops initially wanted to follow the precedent set at Lateran V and exclude them from any active part in the proceedings. The legates intervened. They argued, successfully, that it would be unfitting *(indecens)* not to hear the theologians when the council treated doctrinal issues. But what a proper procedure for hearing them might be was not settled.

At first the legates simply placed bishops and theologians together on deputations dealing with doctrinal issues. The bishops found this system, which immediately exposed their meager theological skills, highly distasteful *(odiosissimum)*. The legates had to find another way to make use of the theologians and restore peace in the assembly.

In late February, they hit upon the solution. They would designate one or more persons, often theologians, to come up with a series of questions on a given issue. They delivered the questions to both the bishops and the theologians. Then the theologians one by one took the floor and presented their views to the assembled bishops, who listened in silence. There was thus no debate in the sense of an ongoing give-and-take but only a serial presentation of judgments on a topic.

By means of this procedure, the Council of Trent incorporated the theologians as a body into the official procedures of the council. The body, called the Congregation of Theologians, functioned as an indispensable institution of the council, even though no official document ever stipulated it as such. No doctrinal issues could move forward without previous vetting by the Congregation of Theologians.

The meetings of the theologians with the bishops lasted for several hours and occurred twice a day, morning and afternoon. They might go on for days, and they concluded only when all the theologians had spoken or the bishops decided they had heard enough. The bishops, now schooled in the subject under discussion, then debated it among themselves and worked toward formulating a draft decree. They consigned the actual formulation of the draft to a deputation specially constituted for that purpose and made up of both theologians and bishops. This set of procedures, which began almost as an experiment in February and March 1546, became standard for the rest of the council.

In November 1546, Emperor Charles V urged through his ambassador at the council a further employment of the theologians. The emperor believed that if the council first undertook a vigorous reform of the church, it would thus ease the political situation in Germany and make feasible an agreement on the doctrinal issues. By November, however, the council was on the threshold of approving a decree on the doctrine of justification, which the emperor feared would only exacerbate the situation in Germany.

He proposed, therefore, that the theological faculties of major universities, such as Paris, Louvain, and Salamanca, approve the decree on justification before the council promulgated it. In itself, this was not an outlandish proposition given the public doctrinal roles such faculties played at the time. The emperor further argued that the approval by the faculties would ensure reception of the decree in the Catholic kingdoms.

The legates summarily rejected the proposal. It was, according to them, too difficult to implement, contrary to church practice, setting a bad example, and superfluous because Paris and Louvain had already condemned Luther. They also rejected the emperor's alternative proposal that the universities send delegations to the council to approve its decrees because it seemed to grant universities an authority greater than that of the council. The emperor pressed the case no further.

Because a plague threatened Trent, the legates transferred the council to Bologna in the spring of 1547. Unlike Trent, Bologna had a university, one of the oldest and most prestigious in Europe. Renowned for its law faculty, the university did not have a faculty of theology as such, but it linked together the "houses of study" *(studia)* of the mendicant orders in the city into a kind of consortium. The influx into the council of theological experts from these institutions made the size of the Congregation of Theologians at Bologna considerably larger than at any other time during the council. On April 29, 1547, for instance, more than eighty were present. They very much outnumbered the bishops.

The *studia* of the mendicants housed large libraries, with just the kind of collections the council needed for its work. The Dominican convent was especially important because talented young members of the order came there from all over Europe to complete their studies. The legates admitted these and theological students from other convents in the city to listen to the Congregation of Theologians until their numbers grew so great that the practice had to be stopped. Over 300 were present, for instance, on April 2.

When the council resumed in 1551 for its second period, the new legate, Marcello Crescenzio, somewhat restricted the role of the Congregation of Theologians, but in the third and decisive period, 1562–1563, the Congregation functioned as it had originally. At Trent, therefore, the theologians played two roles. They were the bishops' teachers when they lectured to them in the meetings of the Congregation of Theologians and thus prepared them for a more informed interaction later among themselves. That was their first role. The theologians also

collaborated with the bishops in hammering out
the substance and the wording of the decrees. That
was their second.

Vatican I

Although in debating who had the right to participate in the council, the Central Commission did not
explicitly discuss theologians, it assumed they would
participate. It decided that a Congregation of Theologians on the model of Trent was not necessary
but made clear that it intended to make full use of
the expertise that only such professionals could
provide.

At the time the Council of Trent met, that city
had no university. Even aside from the strong medieval tradition of the universities sending theologians to councils, Trent would in any case have had
to import them if it wanted them present. Vatican
I, however, met in Rome, where it had at its immediate disposal theologians from the Jesuits' Roman
College, which, despite its name, had university
status. (The institution is now called the Gregorian
University.) The council called into service theologians, canon lawyers, and church historians from

elsewhere, but it relied most consistently on the nearby Jesuits.

In the winter of 1867–1868, the Central Commission urged nuncios and bishops to recommend theologians, canon lawyers, and church historians, from which it chose ten to join the forty already enlisted from Roman institutions. Cardinal Schwarzenberg, the archbishop of Prague, strongly objected to the almost overwhelming predominance among these professionals of those who leaned to ultramontane positions and followed methods he considered outmoded.

The Central Commission responded by throwing a broader and more international net. Though somewhat mitigated, the original ideological bias still prevailed in the ninety-six experts that eventually collaborated in Rome in the constructing of the draft documents. Among them, the sole member from the United States was James A. Corcoran, a priest of the diocese of Charleston, South Carolina, the unanimous choice of the American hierarchy to represent it.

To help in developing the procedures for the council, the Central Commission made use of the local talent of Sebastiano Sanguineti, professor of church history at the Roman College. It then called to Rome Karl-Josef Hefele, professor of church history at the University of Tübingen. Hefele was a highly respected historian of councils. He chafed under the ultramontane atmosphere that he found in Rome. When he shortly thereafter became bishop of Rottenburg, he was able to take an active part in the council itself, where he acted as a strong opponent of infallibility.

Pius at one point considered inviting John Henry Newman as an expert and asked his bishop, William Bernard Ullathorne, to inquire of Newman. The hope among some Catholics that the Oxford Movement, the high-church ferment at the university, would result in a flood of conversions to Catholicism probably prompted the pope's interest in Newman, who was himself a product of the Movement. In any case, Newman demurred on the grounds of poor health and the inability to speak any language except English.

During the council's preparation, theologians took the leading role in preparing the draft documents. About two weeks after the council opened, the bishops received "On the Catholic Faith against the Manifold Errors of Rationalism," which in a drastically revised version the council later approved as *Dei Filius,* "Dogmatic Constitution on the Catholic Faith."

The principal author was Johann Baptist Franzelin, a German Jesuit teaching at the Roman College. The bishops severely criticized the text on several counts, including its abstruse and academic wording. Franzelin defended the text on the grounds that it was directed especially against Catholic "semi-rationalists" teaching in German universities. He argued that since the problem was academic, the language dealing with it had to be academic.

Franzelin convinced his critics that German universities were the source of the problem, which betrayed and helped produce a suspicion of universities in Vatican I that was lacking in Trent. The council's deputation responsible for the revision of the document decided, nonetheless, that even though the problem originated in universities, the language needed to be less academic and more positive. For the revision, it created a subcommission of three bishops that included Konrad Martin of Paderborn. The major burden of the revision fell on Martin because he was the only German of the three. To aid him, he bypassed Franzelin and called instead upon Josef Kleutgen, another German Jesuit from the Roman College.

Universities had the reputation of being tainted with modern philosophies. Moreover, their critical-historical approach to sacred texts seemed destined to destroy any religion based on divine revelation. Guillaume-René Meignan, bishop of Châlons-sur-Marne, addressed the problem in one of the more important interventions on the draft. He had studied Scripture at Munich, Berlin, and Rome, and he was, therefore, fully abreast of what was happening in the field.

Meignan conceded that some scholars used the new methods to advance a rationalistic or even atheistic agenda, but proper use of philology, history, and archeology threw light on difficult biblical passages. Catholic exegetes, therefore, needed freedom and encouragement to pursue such methods. Although Meignan surely did not convince everybody, he seems to have helped moderate the language of the final form of the decree.

Experts worked on drafts of other documents, but the only one besides *Dei Filius* subjected to extensive debate leading to final approval was *Pastor Aeternus.* Once the council took the decision to address primacy and infallibility as a decree separate from the comprehensive draft on the church originally prepared, the deputation had to come up with a text.

It put the task principally in the hands of Clemens Schrader, a Jesuit from the Roman College, and Willibald Maier, personal theologian of Ignaz von Senestrey, bishop of Regensburg. Although somewhat modified in the course of debate, the Schrader-Maier text substantially survived to become the definitive *Pastor Aeternus.*

At Vatican I, therefore, the theologians performed an essential service. They did not, as at Trent, constitute a Congregation of Theologians, a well-defined body formally incorporated into the council's procedures. Their role at Vatican I was, however, at least as important and more directly related to the creation of the council's texts. The major difference between the theologians at Trent and those at Vatican I was how in the latter council the papacy had the major role in determining who they would be.

Vatican II

At Vatican II, the papacy assumed an even more pronounced control. John XXIII had named the cardinal prefects of the Vatican congregations as presidents of all but one of the ten preparatory commissions, and he in principle appointed the members of the commissions, including the theologians. In theory, the theologians were to speak only when asked for their opinion, which was a drastic reduction and even reversal of their role at the Council of Trent. In practice, however, most commissions proceeded informally in a lively exchange among all those present.

A more important distinction was between members and consultors who lived in Rome and those who lived elsewhere. On the former fell the burden of the work to such an extent that cynics referred to the latter as merely honorary members. In the mid-twentieth century, Rome was even richer in institutions for the training of future priests than it had been during Vatican I. The commissions had at hand an abundance of experts.

The distinction between local and distant members had, however, theological implications. Roman institutions had more than their share of theologians ignorant of the new methods being applied to sacred subjects and even inimical to them. The commissions favored such theologians over others even in Rome who were more favorable to the new developments. The latter theologians felt largely excluded especially from the Theological Commission and murmured that the documents emanating from the preparatory process failed to come to grips with issues as they now stood.

Shortly after the council opened, the bishops voted for members of the ten commissions that would function during the council, the equivalents of the preparatory commissions. To those commissions, the pope had the right to appoint further members, as indicated in the regulations for the council published about two months before it opened. Section 9 of the regulations specified that the pope had the exclusive authority to name theologians, canon lawyers, and other specialists as consultors (*periti,* experts) to the commissions.

The first list of *periti,* published on September 28, 1962, contained 228 names. By the time the council closed four years later, the list had grown to some 480 *periti* directly appointed by either John XXIII or Paul VI. As the council moved along, the popes appointed ever more *periti* whose approach promoted the unexpected direction the council was taking.

In the fall of 1962, however, that development lay in the future. At issue was the problem Bishop Meignan had addressed at Vatican I, although it now had a broader scope. As we have seen, the problem exploded in the early years of the twentieth century with the Modernist crisis, and now it confronted the bishops head-on at Vatican II.

The regulations allowed bishops to bring their own *periti* to the council. The regulations made a sharp distinction, however, between these experts and those appointed by the pope. It excluded the former from being present in Saint Peter's during the working sessions of both the council and the commissions. Despite these restrictions, the personal *periti* found ways to make their influence felt.

Cardinal Franz König of Vienna, for instance, brought the Jesuit Karl Rahner, a theologian regarded in Rome with considerable suspicion. Cardinal Josef Frings of Cologne brought the young Joseph Ratzinger. In the weeks before the council opened, Rahner and Ratzinger, working with the blessing of the German bishops, composed an alternative to the official text, *De Fontibus,* "On the Sources of Revelation." When the council opened, they had their text circulated among the bishops. With that, the theologians seized an initiative unlike anything in the previous two councils.

In the eyes of its critics, *De Fontibus* stood for all that was bad in the older theological methods. During its preparation, Cardinal Alfredo Ottaviani, head of the Theological Commission, had offended many by his refusal to allow discussion of alternative methods and approaches. His stance annoyed bishops as well as theologians and rendered them ready publicly to oppose the Commission when the opportunity arose.

The Rahner-Ratzinger text in large measure prepared the way for the confrontation, which happened a few weeks later when *De Fontibus* reached the floor for debate. As mentioned earlier, the text received such severe criticism that an overwhelming majority of bishops voted to replace it with a new text. Pope John's intervention at this moment favored the majority and indirectly favored the new approaches to sacred subjects. The fortress had been breached.

But the conflict was most certainly not over. It continued for the rest of the council in great ways and small, and it embroiled institutions in Rome outside the formal operations of the council. In that regard, the Lateran University and the Jesuits' Pontifical Biblical Institute stood at the opposite ends of the spectrum. During the opening months of the council, a war of words broke out between them, with the Biblical Institute on the defensive for the new methods of exegesis. The situation came to such a pass that in a courtesy visit to the Lateran on October 31, 1963, Pope Paul VI gently but publicly and unmistakably communicated that he expected the faculty and students to cooperate with other Roman institutions and to end their polemic.

Although the conflict continued within the council, the decisive battle had been won with the rejection of *De Fontibus.* The best indication of the seismic shift that had taken place was the determining role now played by theologians who earlier had suffered ecclesiastical censure. Among them was the French Dominican Yves Congar. He enjoyed the status of an official theologian of the council even during the first period but had not been able to make his voice heard in the Doctrinal Commission. By the second period, he was on the way to becoming perhaps the single most important theologian of the entire council. Paul VI named as official *periti* other such theologians, including Rahner and John Courtney Murray.

Moreover, in an informal way such theologians performed a service similar to that of the Congregation of Theologians at the Council of Trent. In the afternoons and evenings in various venues in Rome, they lectured on issues raised in the council. The lectures were open to the public, but large numbers of bishops were often present in the hope of better grasping the implications of the documents facing them. To that extent, the theologians again functioned as the bishops' teachers.

Vatican II is unintelligible without an understanding of the theological underpinnings of its decrees. At Trent and Vatican I, theologians played indispensable roles, yet they did so in service to the theological paradigm in possession. The theologians who prevailed at Vatican II gently overthrew a paradigm whose rudiments the Scholastics of the thirteenth century had set in place, and they led the council into adopting a new one, more historically sensitive, more attentive to subjectivity, and more aware of the findings of modern research. The new paradigm was also consonant with the new literary form the council adopted, and it was to some extent determined by it.

Theologians were indispensable at all three councils. At Vatican II, as at the previous two, they performed as reliable partners with the bishops in the creation of texts, but they did something more, something new. They achieved what they did only because the bishops rallied to their side and were ready to follow their lead. Episcopal support allowed the theologians to take up once again the teaching function they performed at Trent but now with results of stunning import.

6

Laity

T HE FIRST eight general councils, convoked by the emperor or empress of the Roman Empire, were imperial institutions as much as they were ecclesiastical, though at the time no one would have made such a distinction. When in the eleventh century Pope Saint Leo IX began the revitalization in the West of the synodal tradition, lay rulers took part in it as a matter of course. At the Council of Mainz, 1049, for instance, Pope Leo and Emperor Henry III shared the presidency.

To Lateran Council IV, the most important of the medieval councils, Pope Innocent III summoned all the leaders of Christendom. The council opened in 1215 with slightly over 400 bishops and about 800 abbots and priors, but also with representatives of lay magnates that included envoys of Emperor Frederick II and of the kings of France, England, Aragon, Hungary, Cyprus, and Jerusalem. Although most of these representatives were clerics, they represented the interests of laymen.

By this time, as attendance at Lateran IV indicates, kings and kingdoms had clearly and definitively emerged in the West to produce a reality that reduced the emperor to a monarch among monarchs. Nonetheless, the imperial office continued to command immense prestige and, at least in theory, entail special responsibility for the well-being of the church, as exemplified by Sigismund regarding the Council of Constance. Even before the pope published the bull of convocation for Constance, the emperor had issued an edict of his own announcing the opening of the council at the Swiss city on November 1, 1414.

The Council of Trent

In the decades between the outbreak of the Reformation and the opening of the Council of Trent, Charles V, the most consistent and prominent advocate for a council, needed it to ease his political situation, but, as emperor and devout Catholic, he also took seriously his responsibilities to work for the well-being of the church. Although other monarchs, especially the king of France, did their best to scuttle Charles's efforts in that regard, Pope Clement VII showed special finesse in eluding the emperor's pleas to him to convoke a council.

Immediately upon his election as Clement VII's successor, Pope Paul III made clear his determination to call the council, which almost automatically made him a partner with Charles V in the undertaking. He finally agreed with the emperor's demand that the council take place "in German lands," and he therefore agreed, though with great reluctance and misgiving, that it be held in Trent, a city in the Habsburg domains. Moreover, as we saw, he eventually had to accept that reform of the church, Charles's priority for the council, would receive equal treatment with doctrine.

On January 13, 1546, a month after the council opened, the legates, who seemed to assume the council would at least in some measure address both doctrine and reform, asked the prelates in which order they were to address them. Heated debate followed. Bishops aligned with the emperor insisted the council first settle the reform issues, whereas those aligned with the pope insisted on just the opposite. Under pressure from both sides, the council finally decided to treat the issues in tandem. A reform decree was to accompany every doctrinal decree.

This compromise allowed the council to go forward, but the tension remained. It did not come to a head until the winter of 1563, during the council's third period. As we have seen, the council was in the midst of a severe crisis that had begun months earlier over an aspect of the reform of the episcopacy and that had brought the council to a standstill. Pius IV, the pope for this period, received the brunt of the blame for the situation. Since the pope seemed unwilling to budge on the reform question, responsible people turned to Emperor Ferdinand I, Charles's brother and successor, to remedy the situation.

Ferdinand, himself dismayed at the council's inability to function, went into action. He wrote two letters to the pope in words unusually blunt for such correspondence. The letters amounted to a formal and official warning that he as emperor was ready to take action in his capacity as Protector of the Church. Ferdinand insisted that the reform of the church had to go forward and had to begin with reform of the papacy and the papal curia, which were the precise areas that the three popes of the council—Paul III, Julius III, and Pius IV—had reserved to themselves.

At no other point during the council did the authority of the laity more strongly show itself than in Ferdinand's warning to the pope, who suddenly realized that the talk at the council of deposing him might take practical form. The situation was all the more dangerous because King Philip II of Spain and Queen Catherine de' Medici, regent of France, might well join with the emperor. Pius was eventually able to defuse the situation through the appointment as legate of Giovanni Morone, who was able to work out a compromise.

The laity generally exercised their influence at the council in less dramatic ways. Although bishops retained the ultimate decision-making authority, they were for the most part directly or indirectly chosen by the rulers of their respective lands. They came to the council to work for the good of the church, and by and large that is what they did. Nonetheless, they were keenly aware of the concerns of their rulers and were influenced by them.

Interesting in this regard is the role played by women. In the second period, Mary, Queen of Hungary, acting as regent for the Low Countries, sent eight theologians to the council, whereas the pope sent only two. For the last period of the council, Queen Elizabeth of England boycotted it and even in these early years of her reign made sure Catholic bishops of her realm did not participate. At the same time, Mary Queen of Scots, very much wanted to send bishops, but in a sad letter to the council confessed that the situation in Scotland, which had been practically taken over by the Protestants, made it impossible for her to do so.

In France, Catherine de' Medici withheld bishops from the council until, by the fall of 1562, she realized that it was in her best interest to change her policy. She then sent a small delegation—twelve bishops, three abbots, and eighteen theologians under the leadership of Charles de Guise, the Cardinal of Lorraine. Small though the delegation was, the members were of the highest caliber, none more so than de Guise. At the council he played an often decisive role from this point forward.

To ensure that their interests were protected, rulers sent envoys, quasi-ambassadors to the council, who were understood to be full members of the council even though many of them were laymen. The exalted and special status they enjoyed is clearly indicated in the official records of the council, where they are always listed before the bishops and arch-bishops, and just after the legates and the cardinals. When the council finally concluded on December 4, 1563, they as members of the council signed the official record of the decrees along with the prelates. In so doing, they vicariously committed their sovereigns to accept and implement the decrees, thereby making them partners with the bishops and the Holy See in that task.

Upon their arrival in Trent, the envoys sometimes made a solemn entrance into the city. They assumed seats of honor in the council chamber. If they were laymen, they could not vote on the documents, but individually and collectively they at times exercised considerable influence on the proceedings. When they appeared in the council chamber for the first time to present their credentials, they were able to address the council, an important occasion to make known the concerns of their sovereigns.

On June 27, 1562, for instance, Sigismund Baumgartner, a layman, envoy of Albrecht V, duke of Bavaria, arrived for the first time in the council chambers and addressed the assembly. Citing information from an extensive visitation of Bavaria in 1558, Baumgartner painted a dark picture. The majority of the parish clergy was ignorant and infected with heresy. Out of a hundred, all but three or four were either married or openly keeping concubines. The envoy pleaded for implementation of three remedies to prevent the situation from deteriorating further: granting the Eucharistic cup to the laity, enforcing stricter discipline for the clergy, and, as mentioned earlier, granting permission for married men of proven integrity to be ordained. The council listened respectfully but took no action, leaving it to the pope to handle those issues once the council ended.

The council during its second period debated an early version of a decree on the reform of the episcopacy. All the envoys at the council at that time except those from the Republic of Venice and the Duchy of Florence visited the legates to express their displeasure with the decree. According to them, the decree took little account of the real needs of the church and was unworthy of the council. They expressed a sentiment that many bishops at the council also felt. Indicative of the prerogatives the envoys believed they enjoyed was their request at this time to see the text of reform decrees before they were distributed to the bishops.

It was during the final period of the council that the envoys were collectively able to make a palpable display of their authority. Morone, the chief legate, had drawn up a long decree on "the reform of the princes," which was essentially a unilateral rewrite of church-state relations that emphasized the church's exception from secular jurisdiction. It also abolished certain "privileges" the monarchs enjoyed. The envoys and their sovereigns, not surprisingly, found the document unacceptable. They applied so much pressure that they were able to weaken the document into little more than an exhortation to the princes to do their duty.

Vatican I

The Central Preparatory Commission of five cardinals created by Pius IX to advise him on how to proceed with the council held its initial meeting on March 9, 1865. It recommended that "the Christian princes" not be consulted at present but do what was proper in their regard at the time of the official convocation. Pius accepted the suggestion, and with that the princes were promptly forgotten.

Months passed, during which the commission tried to decide, based on precedent, who had the right to participate in the council. Not until the very last minute, when in 1868 the bull of convocation was about to be published, did it discuss whether to invite the princes, and it did so only because the papal Secretary of State, Cardinal Giacomo Antonelli, sounded the alarm. Antonelli realized what a sensitive issue this was and how serious were its political and diplomatic implications.

The curia was well aware that rulers had played a role in previous councils, but it was also aware of how radically the present situation differed from all that had gone before it. The French Revolution had chased princes from their thrones, and even those who were able afterward to claim them back often lost them again. The situation was volatile, as Europe was wracked by revolutions and social unrest. The 1868 revolution in Spain, just at the time the bull was being prepared, drove Queen Isabella II into exile, confirming the widespread persuasion in the curia that the world was now bereft of truly Christian princes.

On June 23, 1868, just six days before the bull's scheduled publication, the commission held an emergency meeting to address the question. The presence at the meeting of both the pope and Antonelli underscored the seriousness of the question. The commission finally decided that the political situation was too unstable, complicated, and unprecedented to allow a formal invitation to heads of state. Nonetheless, in an effort not to break entirely with tradition, the bull would urge the cooperation of governments, without specifying what that might mean. It thus left the door slightly open for participation in some form.

In France, the significance of the failure to invite princes, such as Emperor Louis Napoleon, was discussed at the highest level of government, as was the advisability of the government's availing itself of the cooperation proviso and sending a representative to the council. Like most others in the government, Émile Ollivier, the future prime minister, was against participation. He interpreted the failure to invite princes or other heads of state as an implicit declaration of the separation of church and state—or even a declaration of isolation of the church from lay concerns, which surely the Holy See did not intend.

As things turned out, no government, no matter how it interpreted the proviso, sent a representative, which made Vatican I the first ecumenical council in history without direct lay participation. Even so, the laity was able to have a considerable impact upon the council, most notably as being among the most ardent and most widely influential promoters of the ultramontane movement, which culminated in the definition of infallibility.

Contrary to what is often assumed, Ultramontanism was a grassroots movement that began to gain momentum in 1819 with the publication of Joseph de Maistre's *Du pape.* De Maistre, layman, aristocrat, diplomat, and political theorist, dismayed at what the Revolution had wrought, argued that an infallible papacy was the God-given institution that alone could stabilize society.

Catholics, especially of the upper classes, had suffered terribly as a result of the Revolution and its aftermath, and were therefore susceptible to the kind of message de Maistre delivered, even though they did not necessarily subscribe to every aspect of his vision. In the decades leading up to the council, other laymen took up the pen in favor of a papacy with stronger authority to enforce its discipline and to teach without the possibility of dissent or correction, that is, to teach infallibly. The idea was not new among theologians, but it had never entered into the public square with such force before. Notable among the laymen promoting the movement were Joseph Görres in Germany, Juan Donoso Cortés in Spain, and William George Ward in England.

Of course, clerics also promoted the movement, most especially the Jesuits from the staff of *La Civiltà Cattolica,* the Jesuits' influential journal in Rome. Before Gregory XVI (r. 1831–1846) became pope, he in 1799 published a volume that sounded the first notes in what would become the ultramontane movement. The volume remained almost dormant until his election, after which it got widespread attention and was translated into several languages. Nonetheless, laymen were crucial to the movement's success.

No layman attained a higher profile or exerted a more direct impact on Pius IX than Louis Veuillot (1813–1883), who in 1846 took up the editorship of *L'Univers,* the Parisian journal that he turned into the most strident and extreme ultramontane voice in Europe from that point forward. Born into humble circumstances, Veuillot by dint of talent, determination, and hard work acquired an education and social acceptability. His education included little religious instruction beyond basic catechism, but this deficiency did not deter Veuillot from lecturing and correcting the French bishops who did not share his views.

In the early 1850s, Veuillot engaged in public controversy with them, especially with Dominique-

Auguste Sibour, the archbishop of Paris, the most important see in France, and he did so with the silent acquiescence of the Holy See. He visited Rome on a regular basis, where he was received as a welcome celebrity and won easy access to the pope, who in large measure shared his views. During the council, he set up a household in Rome, where he collected information about the council to transmit to his journal in Paris. In that regard, he had the advantage of being received several times in private audience by the pope, a privilege denied some bishops.

Veuillot and the others were certainly not responsible for the definition of infallibility at Vatican I. It was the bishops who made that decision after long deliberation. Nonetheless, the passionate advocacy of the doctrine by such men and their eagerness to engage in public controversy over it almost inevitably meant that the council would take it up and that, once taken up, would define it.

While Veuillot was in Rome during the council, he surely gave aid and comfort to like-minded prelates, but he seems to have had no direct influence on the council's dynamic. That was not true of Lord Acton (John Emerich Dalberg-Acton), a layman as determinedly opposed to infallibility as Veuillot was in favor of it. During the council, he too set up a household in Rome, which became an important gathering place for "the minority," the prelates who for one reason or another opposed the definition. His family connections gave him access to many circles in Rome, and he soon began to assist the minority in a way that went far beyond providing a comfortable venue.

At the age of sixteen, Acton had presented himself at the doorstep in Munich of Ignaz von Döllinger, the highly respected Catholic church historian, destined to become the best-known and most formidable opponent to infallibility, and asked him to be his mentor. This brilliant young man, a devout Catholic, fluent in English, German, French, and Italian, related by blood or marriage to several noble families on the continent, soon graduated from his student status with Döllinger to become his closest friend.

Acton seems to have moved to Rome for the council principally to supply Döllinger with information he could use to carry on his campaign against infallibility, which is precisely what he did. Acton wrote to him almost every day. To that extent, Acton worked directly to negate the influence of Veuillot and others like him. But Acton, a layman with no official position within the council itself, played a role that affected the council's inner workings.

When prelates opposed to the definition arrived at the council, they discovered to their dismay that they constituted only about 20 percent of the membership. Within the first month, they also discovered that the prelates of "the majority" were much better organized and mobilized. Despite the talent and experience of the prelates of the minority, they seemed incapable of organizing themselves for concerted action. Acton stepped into the vacuum and worked with them to establish effective and coordinated procedures for dealing with the situation.

In a letter of January 24, 1870, Odo Russell, unofficial British ambassador to the Holy See, described how those prelates marveled at Acton's honesty of purpose, clearness of mind, and organizational ability, which had led them to a coherence they had thought impossible. As it turned out, even with Acton's help, the minority consistently found itself playing a catch-up game. Nonetheless, without Acton, their situation would have been worse.

Vatican II

In the preparation for Vatican II, the possibility of a role in the council for heads of state seems to have occurred to no one. The lacuna is perfectly understandable in the context of the times. The Code of Canon Law then in force listed the prelates to be called to an ecumenical council with the right to vote (canon 223). It mentioned no other members of a council. The organizers of Vatican II probably simply followed the provisions of the canon.

Although the church did not yet officially recognize the legitimacy of separation of church and state, a practical separation between them existed in some form in most countries of the Western world. It would have been awkward, if not politically suicidal, for a prime minister or president to send an envoy to assume formal membership in the council.

Moreover, the organizers of Vatican II could rely on the no-prince precedent set by Vatican I. If princes were not to be invited, what were the criteria for inviting other laymen—or laywomen? This was a question difficult to answer and almost certainly not even addressed as the preparations for the council were in progress. Once the council got under way, however, the question of lay participation assumed a certain urgency.

By the early years of the twentieth century, an impressive number of lay organizations were flourishing in the church. In Paris in 1833, for instance, Frédéric Ozanam, a young student at the Sorbonne, organized a few other students to help the poor and thus laid the foundation for the Society of Saint Vincent de Paul. The Society flourished and spread to other cities of France and then to other countries. It was thriving at the time of the council and is still active today.

In the United States, the Knights of Columbus, founded in 1882, and the women's counterpart, the Catholic Daughters of America, founded in 1903, were important, but so were other organizations such as the National Council of Catholic Men and the National Council of Catholic Women, both founded in 1920 by the American hierarchy to promote the lay apostolate (laity working with and for other laity for Catholic causes). Similar institutions functioned throughout the Catholic world. The most important of all, however, was Catholic Action, vigorously promoted by Pope Pius XI (r. 1922–1939), who defined it as "the participation of the laity in the apostolate of the hierarchy."

At the time of the Council of Trent, self-determining lay organizations known as confraternities were almost ubiquitous in the church, but they were isolated units that operated independently of one another even when they were plentiful in a given locality. Moreover, their fundamentally democratic procedures did not generate leaders with long-term tenure and high profile. These features made them less capable of exerting influence beyond their immediate circle. Moreover, the tradition that rulers represent the laity had taken hold at Nicaea and remained unquestioned until political conditions changed so radically in the nineteenth century.

However, from the very beginning of the preparatory phase of Vatican II, a number of Catholic organizations of laypersons strove to make an active contribution to the council. The leaders of Pax Romana, the International Movement of Catholic Intellectuals, for instance, sent a report to the authorities of the council in June 1960, just as preparations were getting under way. The Conference of International Catholic Organizations sent a series of six reports during the preparation period.

The number, importance, and influence of such organizations explain how easily the idea arose for the council to make a statement on the phenomenon. On October 8, 1964, Cardinal Fernando Cento enthusiastically introduced to the council the draft document "On the Lay Apostolate." He made sure to thank especially the laymen and laywomen who had helped in the composition of the document. The document affirmed that the laity had an apostolate in the church, whose sacramental basis was their baptism and confirmation. They participated "in the royal priesthood of Christ and in his mission."

Laypersons had begun to work on the document a year and a half earlier, in February 1963. A precedent had been set. As the council moved along, the precedent began to have an impact. Some hundred laypersons contributed to the fashioning of the council's final document, *Gaudium et Spes*. During the course of that document's long history, moreover, some bishops had submitted the text to laypersons for their comments.

Pope Paul VI, who had been a strong advocate of the laity in Italy before he was pope, took a keen interest in the text "On the Lay Apostolate," and, more important, decided to invite lay auditors to the council, a decision made public on September 14, 1963, on the eve of the opening of the council's second period. He chose twelve laymen as official auditors during that period.

By the third period the number of laymen had increased to twenty-one. During the previous period, Cardinal Léon-Joseph Suenens had noted the anomaly of women's absence from the council hall, and he thereby applied pressure for action. Paul VI responded by appointing seven women from religious orders and seven laywomen, who like the men were auditors at the council.

The influence these auditors had on the council is impossible to calculate, especially since it was informal, carried on for the most part in casual conversations inside and outside the basilica. It was more than token but probably not much more than that. Yet, it did provide a precedent for the laity in councils when there were no longer princes or princesses to speak for lay concerns, and in the Catholic church precedent is important.

7

The Other

As Roman Catholic institutions, councils reserved full membership to Roman Catholics. Nonetheless, others influenced the councils in serious ways and in some instances were even physically present in the council chambers. Any consideration of the important players in such gatherings must take them into account.

It is perhaps stretching a point to include objectivized situations such as the modern world in the category of the Other, but I am going to do so because the dialectic between them and the two Vatican councils is crucial for understanding why the councils took the courses they did and how they became the institutions they turned out to be. Dialectic with the Other—persons or situations—was usually the stimulus for convoking a council and the dynamic that drove it forward once convoked.

The Council of Trent

Without Luther, the Council of Trent would not have happened. Moreover, once the council met, it limited its doctrinal agenda to issues raised almost exclusively by Luther. The council's reform agenda was broader and less directly related, but it nonetheless derived much of its urgency from the crisis Luther had provoked. Emperor Charles V envisaged the council as the last hope for reconciliation with the Lutherans, and he prevailed upon a highly skeptical Pope Paul III to adopt the same attitude. They meant the council to be a council of reconciliation.

If that goal were to be achieved, it required that the Lutherans come to the council. By the 1530s, leadership among the Lutherans had slipped from theologians such as Luther and Melanchthon to princes within the empire, which meant that invitations to the council had to be addressed to them. The princes were now organized collectively into the Schmalkaldic League, a military alliance to defend themselves against the Emperor and his Catholic allies.

In the first year of his pontificate, Paul III announced a council to meet in Mantua, a duchy in central Italy. Mantua was a fief of the emperor, and it therefore technically fulfilled the Lutheran demands that the council be held "in German lands." The pope sent Pier Paolo Vergerio as his nuncio to Germany to win cooperation and ensure participation. Although at the beginning of his mission Vergerio got mixed reactions from both Catholics and Lutherans, he did not deem the cause lost. He was encouraged when he traveled to Wittenberg, where on November 13, 1535, he met Luther. At the meeting, Luther declared himself ready to defend his position at a council either in Mantua or Verona.

The decision lay, however, not with Luther but with the League, which replied to the invitation at its meeting in early 1536. The princes of the League assured the nuncio that they were ready to meet "in a true Christian council in German lands" but that Mantua did not fulfill that condition. There was at Mantua, they said, no guarantee for the safety of the participants. More important, there was no freedom in the council's decisions as long as the pope refused to submit to the council's supreme authority. In other words, the pope, if he were present, would be simply another member of the council, a condition no pope could possibly accept.

The reply set the pattern for the fate of all future invitations. The council opened at Trent on December 13, 1545, therefore, without Luther, who died shortly afterward, and without any of his followers or Lutheran princes. The refusal of the Schmalkaldic League to send representatives to the council gave Charles V the excuse he needed to go to war against it, a project in which he won the pope's cooperation. All thought of reconciliation had obviously flown out the window.

Relations between Charles and Paul deteriorated so badly that it resulted in ending the first period of Trent. When Paul died shortly afterward, his successor, Julius III, reconvened the council, partly as an expression of good will toward Charles. The League, though it had been defeated by Charles, had in the meantime regrouped and reclaimed its leadership position.

In this new situation, Charles hoped that the League, chastened by its defeat, might be willing to soften its conditions—a vain hope. Nonetheless, negotiations continued all the way through this second period of the council and finally had results.

At its Thirteenth Session, October 11, 1551, the council postponed discussion on several points regarding the Eucharist until it could hear the Lutherans' opinion. To that end it published the first of its two guarantees of safe-conduct for them. The document promised, among other things, "full liberty to confer, make proposals, and discuss those things that are to be discussed in the council, and to come freely and safely."

Eleven days later, the council welcomed its first Lutherans, two envoys of the Duke of Württemberg. The envoys decided not to engage the council until more Lutherans arrived. A month later an envoy came from Strasbourg, the renowned historian Johann Sleiden, just in time for the Session on November 25, but both he and the envoys from Württemberg had yet to say an official word. They were there but not there. Meanwhile, envoys from the Duke of Saxony had arrived, as well as six Lutheran theologians. Yet to be decided by the papal legate, Crescenzio, was the mode and measure of participation to be granted them.

On their side, the Lutherans had a big but predictable set of conditions to be met before they took an active part in the council. They demanded that they be given votes equal to those of the bishops, that the decisions already taken by the council be reopened, that the council elect its own presidents (thus displacing the papal legate), and that the pope be subject to the council's decrees. In this way, the council would become a true council.

Pope Julius had told the legate that the Lutherans were to be admitted only if they agreed to submit to the council as it was already constituted. Charles V agreed that the council must not yield its authority, but it could certainly grant the Lutherans a hearing and give them an opportunity to defend their positions. Caught in the middle, the legate hit upon a compromise. He arranged for a semiofficial meeting of the council on January 24, 1552, held outside the usual council chambers. There the Lutherans could present their positions to the bishops but not in a formal meeting of the council.

The meeting duly took place, and at it the Lutherans repeated their by now standard demands. The envoy of Maurice, Duke of Saxony, flung at the assembled prelates the most comprehensive rejection of the council. Trent, he asserted, was not a "general, free, and Christian council" since it was convoked by the pope and had already committed grave errors in doctrine.

During the meeting the bishops remained silent. When the meeting concluded, the secretary of the council announced that after mature deliberation the council would respond. The episode dealt a fatal blow to the council, already badly weakened by internal conflicts and difficult relations with both pope and emperor. The council never responded to the Lutherans, nor did it schedule any further meetings with them. The second period of the Council of Trent unraveled from this point forward, and with it the hope of reconciliation.

It is clearer today than it was in the sixteenth century that by 1552, thirty-five years after the outbreak of the Reformation, the problem was no longer disagreement over this or that doctrine. Lutherans had developed into Lutheranism. They had developed and appropriated an operational paradigm that was incompatible with the Catholic. Lutheranism was now a mature system. The only way a reconciliation could take place was for one of the systems to yield to the other and thereby lose its identity.

There was a further problem, the literary forms in which the two parties expressed themselves. Trent spoke as a legislative body and a court of criminal justice. Its literary forms impelled the council, therefore, to draw firm lines between good and bad, between right and wrong, and they produced a judgmental mind-set, little conducive to a fruitful conversation. But the problem lay not exclusively on the Catholic side. The prophetic, take-it-or-leave-it model of Lutheran discourse, as expressed in categorical assertions and demands, made an impasse inevitable.

The meeting on January 24 was the only time in the history of the council that the two parties directly encountered one another. It failed utterly. Nonetheless, when Pope Pius IV convoked the third period a decade later he sent envoys to the Lutheran princes inviting them to the council. They responded with a firm negative because the pope had no authority to convene such a gathering. In May 1561, the papal nuncio bearing the invitation to the council for Queen Elizabeth in England was denied entrance into the kingdom on the grounds that the presence of nuncios in England was illegal and could lead to unrest. By the time the council reopened, all talk of inviting the Other had vanished, and the council went on to complete its agenda without giving further attention to the matter.

Vatican I

In the 1840s the conversion to Catholicism from the Oxford Movement of such luminaries as John Henry Newman, William George Ward, and Henry Edward Manning, who became the Catholic archbishop of Westminster, made an impression on everyone who followed church affairs. As Vatican I was being prepared, a fair number of bishops and even cardinals began to think that the council might be an occasion to restore church unity. They had little idea how complex the issues were or how unprepared they were to take effective steps in addressing them. Nonetheless, they prevailed upon the Central Commission preparing the council to recommend to Pope Pius IX that he send a letter to the patriarchs of the Orthodox churches and to the Protestants.

Pius readily agreed to do so. In the letter to the Orthodox, he showed little sensitivity to their grievances. Even worse, the letter appeared in the Roman press before it arrived at its destinations. The reaction of the patriarchs was understandably negative. The affair simply confirmed their long-standing prejudices against Rome. There was no possibility that they would respond positively.

If it was clear that the invitation to the Orthodox be addressed to the patriarchs, it was not at all clear to whom the letter to the Protestants be addressed. Moreover, the letter could not convey the impression that the Protestant churches were real churches, since they were only "assemblies of laypersons." Even if they renounced their errors, they still did not qualify as churches. Moreover, with the Anglicans somewhat of an exception, these assemblies did not have a central authority to whom the letter might be addressed. What was to be done?

The commission finally decided to address the letter to Protestants in general. In it, the pope would invite them to reconsider their position and come to realize that the Catholic church was their true home. The commission hoped the letter would stimulate conversions, even if it did not result in the presence of any Protestants at the council.

On September 13, 1868, Pius published *Iam Vos Omnes,* addressed to "all Protestants and other non-Catholics." Although in a few restricted circles it received a respectful hearing, the general reaction was resoundingly negative, and it sparked especially bitter exchanges in Germany. The result was inevitable. Only Roman Catholics entered the council chambers.

What weighed upon the minds of Catholics in the middle years of the nineteenth century was not the religious divisions within Christianity but the profound problems raised by the new and threatening world in which they found themselves. In the wake of the French Revolution, earlier movements and impulses coalesced to produce a reality that upset assumptions and values that had seemed timeless and unassailable.

The dogmas of liberty, equality, and fraternity upset the dogma of hierarchy upon which church and society had rested since the most ancient times. The Scientific Revolution, now ubiquitously pervasive in its influence, rendered obsolete the verities of the physics and cosmology of the ancient world, and new philosophies had displaced Plato and Aristotle from their thrones. The Industrial Revolution effected profound changes in the structure of society, producing a downtrodden proletariat with nothing to lose but their chains. The Enlightenment had thrown history's goal into the future, thus transforming tradition from a source of wisdom and cultural enhancement into an obstacle to progress. Finally, scholars now applied their newly critical-historical methods to every form of tradition, including sacred texts and sacred doctrines, and they conclusively showed that certain doctrines and practices attributed to Christ and the apostles, such as the necessity of confession of sins to a priest, developed centuries later.

Few, if any, Catholics understood the situation in such terms, but that did not hinder them from feeling its impact. They targeted Liberalism as the enemy, a catchall term that stood for a compendium of the problems raised by the modern world. Liberalism meant, therefore, a number of things. Included under its umbrella were rationalism, atheism, democracy, disrespect for authority, disdain for tradition, contempt for religion, and the radical secularization of society. It was to become the Other massively present at Vatican I.

Pius had lashed out against these evils and many others in his *Syllabus of Errors,* 1864. Under ten headings divided into eighty propositions, the *Syllabus* "repudiated, proscribed, and condemned" pantheism, rationalism, socialism, communism, the subordination of the church to the state, the separation of church and state, religious freedom, and much more. The often quoted final proposition is the most global and most revealing. It condemned the idea "that the Roman Pontiff can reconcile himself and come to terms with progress, Liberalism, and modern civilization." The very comprehensiveness of the *Syllabus* reveals the profound sense of alienation Pius and many other Catholics felt by the middle of the century.

Pius convoked the council to deal with the situation. Some Catholics advocated that the council simply ratify the *Syllabus* and thus strike all enemies with one blow. The idea never gained ground in the council, but recognition of the far-reaching implications of the challenges led the planners of the council to prepare a broad review of Catholic practices and institutions as the material of the agenda. The first document to appear on the docket, however, addressed the heart of the threat posed by modern culture, the threat to religious belief itself. The document was the "Dogmatic Constitution on the Catholic Faith against the Manifold Errors of Rationalism."

When first presented to the bishops, the Constitution suffered severe criticism. A drastically revised version was returned some weeks later and was soon accepted and promulgated, the first of the only two documents passed by the council. The document, known by its opening words, *Dei Filius,* represents a mode of thinking that rests upon abstract, ahistorical arguments. Just how effectively it met the problems of the day is open to question.

Its strength lay in that it did not say too much. It did not ratify the *Syllabus*. It did not condemn Darwin or Marx, nor Kant or Hegel. It asserted, moreover, a few basic beliefs that served the church as solid guidelines in a shifting landscape. Among them: God exists and can be known. Religious faith is not unreasonable. Faith enhances life. In the last analysis, reason and faith cannot be at odds.

The council ratified *Dei Filius* on April 24, 1870, and at about the same time agreed that it would next address a document on papal primacy and infallibility. *Pastor Aeternus* was, like *Dei Filius,* a response to the crisis of the modern world, in this case a response to the social and political instability wracking the countries of western Europe, which was, as many Catholics understood it, a result of the erosion of respect for the authority of legitimate rulers.

As we have seen, the impetus for a decree like *Pastor Aeternus* came from the grassroots, not from the Holy See itself. De Maistre's *Du pape* opened the campaign for it. Other authors took up the cause, modified or disagreed with de Maistre's argument, and gave the movement a multifaceted character.

Nonetheless, de Maistre's argument remained broadly influential. According to it, the well-being of human society, so badly imperiled by the Revolution, required an authority whose decisions were not open to discussion or revision. Only an infallible papacy fulfilled that requirement. Only an infallible papacy could save society from the modern world.

On July 18, 1870, the council ratified *Pastor Aeternus*. The previous day France had declared war on Prussia, which created the conditions that allowed forces of the new Italian nation to claim the city of Rome two months later. With that, Pius adjourned the council indefinitely. Vatican I was therefore never able to address the rest of the agenda or make further decisions regarding the relationship of the church to the modern world.

Vatican II

When on January 25, 1959, Pope John XXIII announced his intention to convoke a council, he issued "a cordial invitation to the faithful of the separated communities to participate with us in this quest for unity and grace." From the beginning, therefore, the pope intended that in some form Others would be present at the council. In due time, he established the Secretariat for Promoting Christian Unity under Cardinal Bea to make contact with other Christian bodies and urge them to send "observers" to the council. In contrast to both Trent and Vatican I, the response was, after initial hesitations and skepticism, strikingly positive, due in part to the open nature of the invitation (no conditions set down), in part to the trust Pope John had already won, and in part to the impetus of the ecumenical movement already well under way among Protestant churches.

At any given moment, between fifty and a hundred observers were present at the council. In the first period, for instance, fourteen came from Orthodox churches and forty from Protestant ones. They were able to attend every meeting in the basilica, where they enjoyed especially good seating, close to the main altar, and they had the same access to documentation related to the council as did the bishops. Although they could not intervene in the debates, they met every Tuesday afternoon with representatives from the Secretariat, where they had the opportunity to express their views on the issues currently before the council. The media sought them out for interviews, and they blossomed under the courtesy and attention they received.

Their influence upon the council was indirect and difficult to pinpoint, yet gently effective, and it set a pattern for future efforts to promote mutual understanding. The most palpable and dramatic event in this regard occurred on December 7, 1965, the day before the council formally concluded. Bishop Johannes Willebrands from the Secretariat ascended the pulpit in Saint Peter's and read in French the joint declaration of Pope Paul VI and Patriarch Athanagoras of Istanbul lifting the excommunications of 1054 that produced the Great Eastern Schism. The declaration contained a promise to work toward restoring full communion between the churches.

Three days earlier, Pope Paul VI had presided at an ecumenical prayer service for the observers present at the council at that time. It was held in the Basilica of Saint Paul Outside the Walls, the place where Pope John had announced his intention to convoke a council. At the time of the announcement, few indeed would have predicted that within a few years' time a pope would join in prayer with a group of non-Catholic Christians.

Significant though the presence of the observers was at Vatican II, a pressing awareness of the modern world was even more present and significant. Unlike at Vatican I, most bishops came to Vatican II with full awareness that the modern world, that is, the world in which the church lived, had not disappeared, and they realized that in some measure it affected every aspect of the church's life, practice, and teaching. The modern world was not a reality "out there," not a reality separate from the church, and not a reality that the church could chase away. The bishops knew that somehow the council had to address it.

At first implicitly and then more deliberately and intentionally, the council did precisely that. Although the process culminated in the council's final document, *Gaudium et Spes,* "On the Church in the Modern World," it was operative from the very beginning. *Every* document of the council is in some measure a document about "the church in the modern world."

In the century that intervened between Vatican I and Vatican II, the seismic changes that shook traditional verities in the nineteenth century continued on a seemingly inexorable course. The definition of papal infallibility did not have the hoped-for impact upon them. New developments, negative and positive, now posed further challenges. The end of colonialism, for instance, forced the

church, traditionally European, to face a global
and multicultural reality newly assertive. The blood-
iest and most destructive half-century in the history of the human race raised deeply troubling
questions about the future of humanity. World
War II had ended with the explosion of two atom
bombs, which raised the specter of nuclear anni-
hilation. The horrors of the Holocaust laid bare
the depths of depravity and cruelty to which the
modern world had descended and in which, some
argued, the Christian churches had been silently
complicit or worse.

These and similar events had changed the temper
of the modern world from what it was in the nineteenth century. They caused that world to lose its
confidence in the unlimited progress of humanity
and induced other changes in attitude and policy,
some of which now allowed the church to come to
terms with it. In postwar Europe, for instance, the
leaders in the Christian Democracy movement were
Roman Catholic laymen—Konrad Adenauer in
Germany, Alcide De Gasperi in Italy, Robert
Schuman and Charles de Gaulle in France. These
men, devout in their faith, took for granted freedom
of the press, freedom of religion, and some form of
separation of church and state.

Pope John took account of this turn in his address opening the council on October 11, 1962, when he pointedly rejected the view of those who saw "in modern times nothing but prevarication and ruin." He specifically noted that the present political order had in some instances created better conditions "for the free action of the church." Without forgetting the prophetic mission of the church, the council should strive to show the church as "the loving mother of all, benign, patient, full of goodness and mercy towards all those separated from her." The church was to extend a healing and reconciling hand to a proud yet desperately needy world.

There is no more striking proof of how attuned the bishops were to the pope's mandate than the "Message to the World" they issued on October 20, 1962, just nine days after the council opened. The message, utterly unforeseen in the preparations for the council and utterly unprecedented in the history of councils, arose spontaneously from the membership, a precious window into the mind-set with which the bishops from the very beginning viewed their task.

The document was brief. In the name of the council, it gave voice to the message of mercy, kindness, and human compassion that Pope John hoped the council would express. "We urgently turn our thoughts to the problems by which human beings are afflicted today. Hence, our concern goes out to the lowly, the poor, and the powerless. . . . As we undertake our work, therefore, we want to emphasize whatever concerns the dignity of the human person and whatever contributes to a genuine community of peoples."

The message proved to be an adumbration of the direction the council would take. The council was to be a council of reconciliation, which was consistently expressed in its vocabulary with words such as friendship, cooperation, colleagueship, mutuality, and dialogue. Amid the council's daunting complexity, its reconciliatory dynamic imbued it with a remarkable coherence.

In the very first document of the council, *Sacrosanctum Concilium,* "On the Sacred Liturgy," the council sought to reconcile the church to the new global and multicultural reality of the world by validating the inclusion of non-Western traditions in the liturgy. Chapter 3 of *Lumen Gentium,* "On the Church," sought to heal the relationship between the papacy and the episcopal college, a relationship fraught with problems since the Great Western Schism. Other decrees are susceptible to a similar analysis.

In that regard, two documents merit special mention. The decree "On Ecumenism," *Unitatis Redintegratio,* made it through the council with remarkable ease, surely due to a large extent because of the presence of the observers. But their presence testified to the new conditions of society brought about by the effective end of the confessional state and the resulting circumstances in which persons from different churches lived side by side and learned to esteem one another. In such circumstances, the scandal of a divided Christianity cried out for attention and healing.

No Jews were physically present at Vatican II, yet they were virtually present from September 1960, when Pope John ordered Cardinal Bea to prepare a statement on the relationship of the church to the Jews in preparation for the council. Earlier that month, the pope had received in audience the Jewish scholar Jules Isaac, who had laid out for the pope the history of anti-Semitism and its relationship to the Holocaust. This was the remote origin of *Nostra Aetate,* "On Non-Christian Religions." As the title indicates, the document eventually expanded to include others besides Jews, especially Muslims. Unlike the decree on ecumenism, this one had a difficult journey through the council but eventually succeeded to win an overwhelming ratification.

Gaudium et Spes also had a difficult journey, mostly because it was so unprecedented. There were no models that could help its authors fashion it. At the last moment, however, some bishops and theologians objected to its being too contingent, too responsive to "the signs of the times." The objection had merit, but it missed the point that attending to the signs of the times was the very point of the document, which was to address the world and its needs as the world in fact existed, here and now, and to descend from the icy heights of abstraction to respond to human lives as they were really being lived. The document teaches that if the church is to be true to itself it must be concerned about social justice, the destructiveness of modern war, the blessings of peace, and the need to foster respect for the Other. It is addressed not to Catholics, not to Christians, not to believers, but to all persons of good will. It is addressed to the Other, whom by that very fact the church sees as in some measure no longer other.

PART THREE

Impact and Future

8

What Difference
Did the Councils Make?

Each of the three councils had an impact on the church that resulted in significant changes. Beyond that bland platitude, the impact is often difficult to weigh and almost impossible to disentangle from the cultural and sociopolitical context in which it happened. The councils were complex happenings, so we should not be surprised that their impact was complex. Virtually every generalization made about such impact needs qualification. In a chapter as short as this one, generalizations have another major limitation: they can deal with only a highly selective sample of what happened after a council's closing bell rang.

Nonetheless, the generalizations are helpful and need to be made. At a minimum, they raise issues and provide a starting point for further analysis and assessment. At best, they articulate and help identify major assumptions underlying the culture of a given era. For that reason alone, these councils cannot be consigned simply to the category of church history. They were major cultural events.

The cultural ferment in which a council took place provided the overall framework in which the council undertook its deliberations, and it provided, sometimes only in embryo, the issues that formed the council's agenda. This is a crucial point. Unlike the Lord God in the first chapter of Genesis, councils did not begin with a void. They had an already existing reality thrust upon them, and it was in relationship to that reality that they acted and reacted in a variety of ways.

The councils sometimes ratified and gave impetus to a movement already well under way. They at other times unwittingly enabled a development to take place that they had not professedly dealt with. Their more important decisions almost inevitably had consequences, for better or for worse, which they did not foresee or intend. Sometimes an important issue, such as papal primacy at Trent, was too controversial to win a place on the agenda. Sometimes such an issue got passed over simply because it fell outside the purview the council had adopted.

Once concluded, councils had no further control over who would interpret and implement their decisions, and they often had to endure criticism for things they never did. Once a council's decisions entered the give-and-take of the historical process—and all decisions perforce entered that process—they were reshaped and refashioned according to the milieu in which they were received. Some decrees became dead letters almost before they hit the printing press. Others had a brief moment of glory and then slipped into oblivion, perhaps to be resurrected by a later generation and given a renewed importance and impact. A few were immediately and lastingly influential.

The Council of Trent

Without apportioning competencies, the Council of Trent indicated three centers for the interpretation and implementation of its decrees. In one of its very last acts, it reminded "all princes" of their duty to see that the council's decrees be "devoutly received and faithfully observed." Such a mandate was possible only in an age before the nineteenth century, when in many countries of the West either a secularizing government was in power or some degree of separation of church and state had taken place.

In almost the same breath as the mandate to princes, the council stipulated that, should a difficulty arise about the interpretation of a decree, the Holy See was to take measures to resolve it. Finally, in its reform decree on bishops, it had mandated that every bishop hold a synod annually to regulate affairs of the diocese and, quite specifically, to receive and implement the decisions of the Council of Trent.

After the council, these three centers acted both as partners and as rivals regarding the council. In Spain and the Spanish dominions, King Philip II assumed a determining role. He brooked no opposition to his program from a mere bishop, not even the bishop of Rome. But in Milan, though it was under Spanish domination, Cardinal Carlo Borromeo through his diocesan and provincial synods reduced the generalities of the council's decrees to highly specific directives for both the clergy and the laity. When the results of his synods were published as the *Proceedings of the Church of Milan,* they provided a powerful interpretation of how to make the council's decrees practical and operative, and they had an impact on bishops everywhere in the church.

The *Proceedings* became almost indistinguishable from the council's actual decrees.

The papacy saw itself as the principal agent in implementation and interpretation, and it could call upon the council itself to justify that role. The council had committed to the papacy, for instance, several tasks it did not have time to complete, such as a new edition of the Index of Forbidden Books and critical editing of the missal and the breviary. Fulfilling these tasks led to the creation in 1571 of the Congregation of the Index and in 1588 the Congregation of Rites, permanent bureaus that soon claimed absolute authority in their respective areas.

Of even wider import was the Congregation of the Council that Pope Pius IV created immediately after Trent concluded. It continued to expand its remit so as to assume responsibility as the official and final arbiter on the legitimacy of every interpretation and implementation of the council's decrees. It was not disbanded until 1966, a year after the conclusion of Vatican Council II.

When Pius IV established the Congregation of the Council, he also forbade the printing of commentaries or notes on the council's decrees without the explicit permission of the Holy See. In the decades after the council, moreover, the papacy used its effective network of nuncios to make its view prevail as issues arose in different nations and territories.

As mentioned in Chapter 4, Pope Sixtus V in 1588 completely reorganized the Roman curia into fifteen congregations, the equivalent of departments of state. He thus created one of the first modern bureaucracies. This is a good example of how a council's measures helped catalyze a development altogether unintended by the council. The Congregation of the Council and the Congregation of the Index, along with the earlier (1542) Congregation of the Holy Office of the Roman Inquisition, provided the first building blocks for Sixtus V's edifice.

The measures undertaken by rulers, bishops, and popes to interpret and implement the council had considerable impact, yet they got reinterpreted, refashioned, and sometimes nullified by the circumstances in which they were received. Upon the urgent petition of Emperor Ferdinand I and Duke Albrecht V of Bavaria, for instance, Pius IV granted the Eucharistic cup to the laity in their realms, a decision the council had handed over to him. But by that time the cup had become such a powerful sign of differentiation between Catholics and Protestants that after a short while the indult had to be withdrawn. The council's decree forbidding dueling had no impact. It flew in the face of social conventions too deeply entrenched.

The decree *Tametsi* that stipulated that henceforth the church would consider no marriage between Catholics as valid unless witnessed by a priest "in open church" received at first only spotty implementation. In time, however, it gained force and became a requirement that Catholics took for granted and conformed to without second thought. The decree substantially refashioned marriage practices common before the council, and, as the exchange of vows became incorporated into the liturgy of the mass, it imbued Catholic marriage ceremonies with a distinctive character.

As the decades and the centuries passed, several of the council's reform decrees took on an immense importance. The first was certainly the decree in the Twenty-Third Session requiring that bishops reside in their dioceses and pastors in their parishes. Although the decree was not as strong as ardent reformers wanted, the long debate on it ensured that no bishop could leave the council thinking that residency was nothing more than a stipulation of canon law, easily dispensed with. Nonetheless, had it not been for the strong example given by a handful of exemplary bishops after the council, such as Borromeo in Milan and Gabriele Paleotti in Bologna, the mere letter of the law might have remained as ineffectual as earlier decrees on residency had been.

The council also handed bishops a clear job description. Bishops were to visit the institutions of the diocese, they were to see that church buildings be kept in repair, and they were, as mentioned, to hold annual synods. These were tasks traditional to the episcopal office as specified in canon law, but the council marshaled them and thus gave them new force. One of the most important items of the job description, however, was the new mandate for each bishop to establish a seminary in his diocese for the training of poor boys aspiring to the priesthood. Here the council acted as a catalyst in universalizing an institution already in operation in a few places. It had in mind an extremely modest training center, a fallback alternative for boys or young men who could not do better.

These seminaries became a standard feature on the ecclesiastical landscape, but they were destined to have a difficult and very uneven history. Some emerged as exemplary in the quality of the instruction and overall training, but most fell far short of that ideal. They perhaps achieved their best forms only in the middle years of the twentieth century. Nonetheless, despite their problems and often glaring inadequacies, they raised the educational level of a large number of clerics and must be numbered among the successes of the council.

In a hasty, last-minute reform decree, the council affirmed the legitimacy and usefulness of sacred images. It ordered that churches and other places be adorned with them. In this afterthought decree, the council unwittingly made a cultural statement that helped solidify a crucial aesthetic difference between Catholicism and most churches of the Reformation. Nonetheless, only because the Catholic church held sway in the two most generative centers of art production in Europe—Italy and Flanders, soon to be followed by Spain—was the decree to have the ultimate significance it did.

Trent's doctrinal decrees fall into two major categories—the decree on justification (and Original Sin) and the decrees on the sacraments. Although the decree on justification had many merits, it was too long and complex to have direct impact except in the generic sense of being perceived as anti-Luther. Some interpreters argue, however, that the decree's insistence on the necessity of active cooperation with grace helped imbue post-Reformation Catholicism with its dynamism.

The decrees on the sacraments, basically confirmations of medieval speculation on them, reinforced the strongly symbolic and performative character of Catholic worship and understanding of the nature of religion. They were thus consonant with the decree on images. The interiors of Catholic churches were notably different from the interiors of most Protestant churches, and they made evident that between Catholicism and Protestantism the divide was as deeply cultural as it was religious.

After the council ended, even Catholics who had derided it during its long and difficult history rallied to it and identified themselves with it. This development helped give Catholics a sharper sense of identity and of common front against the threat of the Reformation. The council thus contributed unwittingly to the development of the confessional state and thereby to the political divide that marked Europe for centuries to come. That the council contributed to both the cultural divide and the political divide that took ever firmer shape was another of the council's great ironies. Trent, originally convoked with the hope of reconciliation, became an emblem and an instrument of alienation.

Although all the Protestant churches rejected papal authority outright, the council did not issue a decree *De Romano Pontifice* because the bishops at Trent could never have agreed on it. All bishops present at Trent believed in papal primacy, otherwise they would not have been there, but disagreement was rife over what its scope and limits might be. This is a glaring instance of an important issue too hot for a council to handle.

The council also had not a word to say about the great missionary ventures in the New World, certainly one of the most important aspects of Catholicism in the era, whose lasting impact was immense. The council did not address it because it never occurred to the bishops or the legates that it was any of its business. Missions were the business of the mendicant orders such as the Dominicans and Franciscans and of the rulers who supported them. Only in 1622 when Pope Gregory XV created the Sacred Congregation for the Propagation of the Faith did the papacy itself assume a systematic and proactive role in that regard.

When considered as a totality, Trent's decrees had the larger significance of drawing clear lines of demarcation between Catholicism and the churches of the Reformation. The result is ironic, in that both

Charles V and, reluctantly and skeptically, Pope Paul III conceived the council as an instrument of reconciliation. The times simply were not ready for achieving such an urgent goal.

Protestants rejected the council absolutely because its papal sponsorship rendered it illegitimate in its very essence. They paid scarce attention to it and, with few exceptions, proceeded as if it never happened. But Protestants were not the only ones to reject the council. As mentioned earlier, Paolo Sarpi's history of the council interpreted Trent altogether negatively. It convinced at least some Catholics that Trent was a fraud.

Vatican I

In contrast with the large number of decrees issued by both Trent and Vatican II, Vatican I issued only *Dei Filius* and *Pastor Aeternus,* both doctrinal decrees. Both were statements against the modern world. Vatican I thus stood as a symbol and standard-bearer for all those in the nineteenth century who were bewildered and frightened by the great changes taking place before their eyes and who looked for remedies that would provide them with stability and certainty amid a seemingly inexorable flux. In the nineteenth century, modernity no longer meant simply the way things currently were but had become an ideology. In reacting against it negatively, Catholicism took on the guise of its reverse-image ideology.

Even as the council assumed an antimodernity stance, it was itself a remarkably modern happening. For the first time in history, bishops from the remotest parts of the world were able to participate, which was possible only through modern means of transportation. On a deeper level, the centralization of authority promoted by *Pastor Aeternus* was an ecclesiastical version of the centralization taking place in the secular sphere. In the church, this process resulted in a very modern standardization of procedures, as is most obvious in the elimination or significant curtailing of local liturgical practices and in 1918 by the publication for the first time ever of a Code of Canon Law for the entire church.

At the same time, the centralizing impulse called Catholics out of their provincialism into a more expansive vision of the church and, consequently, of the world. It was, to that extent, an early prelude and stimulant to contemporary global awareness. It helped make Catholics more catholic.

The council gave no directions regarding agents or modes of interpretation and implementation. But the very fact of a decree on primacy and infallibility suggests that the Holy See held all authority over the meaning and practical significance of the decrees. Although that interpretation largely explains what happened after the council, controversies in the trenches played a large role in formulating an interpretation that became more or less a consensus. It was an interpretation that rejected the extreme understanding some ultramontanes proposed for *Pastor Aeternus.* When for instance the German bishops responded publicly to the extreme interpretation Chancellor Bismarck gave the decree, Pius IX felt compelled to agree with them and follow their lead.

Dei Filius, the decree on the relationship between faith and reason, made its way easily through the council. It reflected what the bishops had learned in their seminary days and contained a message they all thought necessary for the age in which they lived. As mentioned, it provided a solid center for the church amidst the confusing intellectual currents of the times and was especially important in the positive appreciation it conveyed of the relationship between faith and reason, that is, between Christianity and human culture.

The long-range impact of *Pastor Aeternus* imbued papal statements with a new dignity and doctrinal weight, even when they made no claims to being infallible. But the decree did not turn back the tide of history, and it made no palpable inroads into the political developments of society at large as its promoters had hoped. Outside Catholicism, the decree was largely irrelevant, but on occasion it broke into public controversy, most notably in the United States when in 1960 John Kennedy ran for the presidency. No Catholic could be president, it was said, because he had to accept what the pope pronounced and be more loyal to him than to the American people.

Within Catholicism, it was not in infallibility but in primacy where the most palpable and significant developments took place, not without a certain irony: as the papacy's direct political authority decreased, its ecclesiastical authority increased. There can be no doubt that after the conclusion of Vatican I, the papacy assumed ever greater authority over virtually every aspect of church life. But how much of that gain can be attributed to *Pastor Aeternus* and how much to factors outside the church's direct control is the question.

Of absolutely capital importance in that regard is the almost untrammeled control the papacy assumed after the council over the appointment of bishops. Beginning in the Middle Ages, secular rulers played an important, often determining, role in such appointments, a tradition that in time came to be regulated by concordats between the papacy and the rulers. Although there were tensions, conflicts, and sometimes notorious abuses, the system was not altogether without merit. Things began to change after 1870—not because the church had changed but because the political system had begun to change.

When by 1870 the new Italian monarchy had absorbed into itself the smaller states in Italy, the concordats with those states that gave the state a say in episcopal appointments became dead letters. This new situation provided the papacy with an unanticipated opportunity to act unilaterally in episcopal appointments, with relatively minor oversight by the new Italian government. In seven months between 1871 and 1872, Pope Pius IX chose 102 new bishops, thus filling half the dioceses of Italy. In 1905, the French government unilaterally abrogated the Concordat of 1801, which had given the French government the authority to nominate bishops. Pope Pius X denounced the act but now had a free hand in the appointment of French bishops. And so it went until the process was virtually complete by the middle of the twentieth century. The pope's exclusive right to appoint bishops is now taken for granted, as if it had always been thus.

Beginning in 1819 with de Maistre's *Du pape,* the ardent promoters of infallibility showed that in the modern world a 180-degree turn in social consciousness could be effected in a remarkably short time if the social and political situation somehow supported it. In the eighteenth century, most bishops and leading Catholic thinkers held a much more bishop-centered understanding of church governance and teaching authority than that expressed in *Pastor Aeternus.* The shift within just a few decades was dramatic, as most bishops and thinkers became ultramontane.

Even for ordinary Catholics, the popes achieved a strikingly new prominence in their awareness. After the seizure of Rome in 1870, Pope Pius IX retired to the Vatican quarter of the city and declared himself a prisoner in it, as did his successors until the Lateran Treaty of 1929, which established the independent state of Vatican City. The popes' imprisonment in the Vatican, self-imposed though it was, called attention to them and aroused sympathy among Catholics worldwide. The invention of photography, radio, television, jet travel, and the Internet incalculably intensified awareness of the pope and the papacy. Ordinary Catholics came to recognize the pope's face, know his name, and accept that he "runs the church." That was new.

Vatican II

Vatican II had an immediate impact on the church incomparably greater, faster, and more immediate than any of its predecessors. Unlike those councils, the ordinary faithful could through radio, television, and fast newsprint follow the council on almost a daily basis. More important, they felt its impact in a dramatic way even before the council ended. On the first Sunday of Advent, 1964, most Catholics were startled when they went to mass to discover that large portions of it were now in the vernacular. A rite many believed unchangeable had changed, seemingly overnight, and changed in a drastic and undeniable way. Everybody knew the council was responsible.

The decrees of previous councils had directly affected only the leaders of church and society and had affected the rank and file only in a trickle-down process. Vatican II was in that regard altogether different. The change in the mass was only the beginning. Catholics were now encouraged, for instance, to pray with persons of other Christian denominations, a practice strictly forbidden until the council. They could even attend funerals and marriage ceremonies in other churches, something they previously could do only with the local bishop's permission.

Such changes can stand as symbols for all the other particular changes that took place after the council. Some, though in a broad sense due to the council, were only indirect results of it. Among them was how nonclerics began to obtain degrees in theology and thus notably modify the makeup of the profession. This could be considered a new mode of the lay apostolate. Important though changes like these were, they distract us from the larger perspectives needed to understand the full impact of Vatican II. We must therefore leave such particulars behind and rise to higher perspectives.

We need to realize, for instance, that the council had a considerable impact on other churches and generally resulted in their taking a less negative attitude toward Catholicism, which included a willingness to engage in dialogue with Catholic groups. The constitution "On the Sacred Liturgy" led some churches to restore weekly communion services and revise their liturgical texts; *Nostra Aetate* provided a model for those churches in expressing their relationship to Jews and Muslims; and other enactments of the council also affected other churches.

Within the Catholic church itself, three interrelated changes already stand out as being of overriding importance. The first, the most basic, and the most expansive is how the council's decisions strove to respond to the fact that the church is a reality living in the world and not living in some timeless space. Every document of the council is a document on the church in the modern world. That is the framework that conditions them and that explains the stance they take on the issues under consideration. Every document needs to be read as an expression of the church's struggle to come to terms with the modern world while at the same time remaining faithful to a Gospel proclaimed long ago.

Like the bishops at Vatican I, the bishops at Vatican II realized they were in a cultural, political, and social situation that had no precedent in human history, a situation that challenged the foundations upon which church and society had securely rested. Unlike the bishops at Vatican I, however, the bishops at Vatican II were convinced the clock could not be turned back. The modern world was a reality, on-going and dynamic, with which the church had to come to terms. Moreover, the two world wars, the Holocaust, and other events had shattered some of the most cherished dogmas of Liberalism and modernity, making it possible for the church to recognize and promote positive features in the new situation.

This constituted another 180-degree shift in social consciousness, a shift in how the church related to everything outside it. Of course, in its actual dealings, the church had always and perforce accepted as a given the world around it and had dealt with it in constructive ways. On a deeper level, especially since the thirteenth century, the church, unofficially and not always consistently, had operated on a grace-perfecting-nature paradigm, articulated most pointedly by Thomas Aquinas. That is, it had operated on the assumption of a friendly relationship between the church and human culture, an assumption codified and made official in *Dei Filius* of Vatican I.

Nonetheless, since the nineteenth century and despite *Dei Filius,* the official stance was largely prophetic and anti-world. The *Syllabus of Errors* (1864) had codified the stance into policy. The campaign against the Modernists turned the policy into action. In the decades between then and Vatican II, the anti–modern world policy, though selectively mitigated, remained strong. Vatican II decidedly reversed it and implicitly set a Thomistic reconciliation in its place. There is no more conclusive proof of how fully the council adopted that stance than when *Gaudium et Spes* taught the mutuality of the relationship between "the church and the world" (nn. 40, 44).

The second pervasive reorientation resulting from the council was the new centrality of social issues in Catholic ethical thinking and action. This reorientation sprang most immediately from *Gaudium et Spes,* "On the Church in the Modern World," and from *Dignitatis Humanae,* "On Religious Liberty." It sprang less immediately but most powerfully from the social encyclicals of recent popes—Leo XIII's *Rerum Novarum* (1891), Pius XI's *Quadragesimo Anno* (1931), and John XXIII's *Pacem in Terris* (1963), which was the first papal encyclical ever to be addressed "to all persons of good will."

Well before the council, Catholic moralists recognized the importance of the social encyclicals, but they did not see them as intrinsic to their profession. They dealt with the implications of the Ten Commandments for the life of the individual believer, especially as the priest faced the believer in confession and the believer as he faced the priest. Both confessor and penitent were focused on personal behavior and misbehavior. In this perspective, social issues as such played no role in Catholic moral theology.

But the encyclicals could not be ignored, especially in the training of future priests. The solution often hit upon in seminaries was to relegate them to a special course, usually worth a single academic credit and taught as part of the philosophical (not theological) curriculum. This marginal role began to change as the council was in progress. The "Message to the World" that the council published in the early days of the first period signified a new centrality for social issues in the church's awareness. Then Pope John published *Pacem in Terris* between the first and second periods, thus directly confronting the council fathers with its social message.

A major turning point came on October 4, 1965, when during the council's fourth period Pope Paul VI addressed the United Nations. This was an unprecedented occasion, the first time a reigning pope had set foot in the New World and only the third time a pope had left the Vatican for a foreign country since 1870. All eyes were on Paul VI. He did not disappoint. His message was simple, direct, and delivered in elegant French. It was about social issues, the most basic of which was the necessity of cooperation among nations to secure the common good of all peoples insofar as that was possible. Of great importance was his emphasis on human rights, a theme of the encyclicals, but the high-profile situation of the UN made it striking almost beyond compare.

Paul was able to make a human rights plea because the council, after a difficult and passionate debate, had in principle just ratified *Dignitatis Humanae* with its assertion that freedom of religious choice was a human right. Paul therefore said to the United Nations, "What we proclaim here is the rights and fundamental dignity of human beings—their dignity, their liberty, and above all their religious liberty." A few years earlier such a statement from a pope would have been unthinkable.

The most moving and emphatic moment came when Paul spoke of the horrors of war and of the absolute necessity of world peace. With deep emotion in his voice, he pleaded, "No more war! War never again! It is peace, peace that must guide the destiny of the peoples of the world and of all humanity." The speech was inspired by *Dignitatis Humanae* and *Gaudium et Spes*.

A turning point for the Catholic church and for the church's face to the world had been reached. In the decades since the council, social issues have moved from the margin to a major place in Catholic moral theology. More important, the church has emerged as one of the most consistent and forceful voices in the world pleading for peace, compassion, religious liberty, and human rights. This is a massively important development for both the church and the world. In a newly emphatic way, the popes extended the flock with whose fate they were vitally concerned beyond the Catholic faithful. Pope Francis's encyclical *Laudato Si'*, "On Care for Our Common Home," is a striking example of the new role for the papacy resulting from the council.

If after Vatican II the Catholic church emerged as a major voice promoting human rights, it also emerged as the most conspicuous and important voice urging reconciliation among religious traditions. The church became an agent in promoting it. This is the third great orientation the council effected. It was another 180-degree turn, due directly to *Unitatis Redintegratio*, "On Ecumenism," and especially to *Nostra Aetate*, "On Non-Christian Religions." The latter document provoked some of the acridest and almost desperate debate in the course of the council, a sure indication of how radical it seemed and how important.

Until the council, the church had abstained from the ecumenical movement, and, indeed, Pius XI had condemned it in 1928 in the encyclical *Mortalium Animos*. Pius XII did the same in less stringent terms in 1950 in the encyclical *Humani Generis*. Nonetheless, by the time of the council, Catholics were involved in ecumenism in limited ways, and the Holy See itself had taken a less negative stance. For that reason, *Unitatis Redintegratio* made its way through the council relatively easily, even though it marked a significant turn in attitude and practice and had important theological ramifications.

It was, however, *Nostra Aetate* that made the biggest impact on the church. It gave Catholics a new job description. They were now to be agents of reconciliation among the religions of the world. No more crusades! Indeed, no more belittling other religions or persecuting their faithful. On the contrary, Catholics needed to make every effort to understand them and work with them for the good of society at large. That need was to play a newly central role in how they understood their call to holiness.

While the council directed all members of the church to act as agents of reconciliation, the duty fell especially on the popes. In that regard, John Paul II and now Pope Francis have sometimes been dramatic in the gestures they have made and the actions they have taken. While he was still archbishop of Buenos Aires, Pope Francis entered into an ongoing public dialogue with Rabbi Abraham Skorka, later published as a book. Never in the entire annals of Christian history had a Catholic prelate ever engaged in such an encounter.

Reconciliation is the impulse behind all three of these major changes that the council effected. It is the basic impulse animating Vatican II, and it is a major clue for understanding the council as a whole, a way of rising above specific measures to see the overall orientation of the council. It pins down that sometimes slippery reality known as "the spirit of the council."

Moreover, when an organization undertakes new tasks, especially tasks that entail reversing or radically modifying earlier modes of self-presentation, it to some extent redefines itself. We are what we do. The new tasks Vatican II imposed on the church resulted in a new self-understanding that was both continuous and discontinuous with the past.

9

Will There Be Another One?

ANY ATTEMPT to imagine the future of ecumenical councils in the Catholic church must take at least five factors into account: the size of the gathering, its membership, its location, the potential impact upon it of electronic technologies, and the ancient tradition of collegial governance of the church by the bishops in union with the pope.

As Vatican II was being prepared, the Catholic church numbered about 2,600 bishops with a right to attend. If the same criteria for invitations were used today, more than double that number would have the right. The number of bishops actually present in Saint Peter's during Vatican II normally ranged from about 2,100 to 2,250. Besides them, the basilica had to accommodate hundreds of officially designated theologians, the observers, secretaries, ushers, and other personnel essential for the smooth functioning of the proceedings.

These numbers did not fill the basilica, but they filled the nave. Thus no bishops sat in the side aisles or the transepts, where their view would be obstructed and their sense of belonging reduced. For carrying on a meeting in an equitable way, therefore, Saint Peter's was pretty much at its capacity. If there was absolutely no better alternative, however, Saint Peter's might somehow be outfitted to try to hold the larger number of bishops.

Within the Vatican, there is the Paul VI Audience Hall that seats 6,300, but its suitability as it currently stands for a meeting like an ecumenical council is questionable. Major renovations would be needed, much more extensive than those required to outfit Saint Peter's for Vatican II. Nonetheless, the auditorium is a possible venue—but only if the next council follows the proportion of bishops to others that prevailed in Vatican II.

Given the principle of inclusion that emerged in Vatican II, might not others besides bishops be given a greater physical presence in the council? Bishops, we assume, would retain their traditional voting prerogatives, but might not laymen and laywomen be included to speak for their interests? As we have seen, such lay participation would hardly be an innovation.

In that regard, we need to note that at Vatican II every one of the almost five hundred theologians accredited to the council was a priest. Today nuns and laypersons make up a sizeable proportion of the theologians in the Catholic church. If theologians are to play a role in the next council, they can hardly be restricted to clerics. In that way, it seems, women religious and laypersons would make their voices heard.

Vatican II broke new ground in admitting observers from other Christian churches, which happened before *Nostra Aetate,* "On the Church's Relation to Non-Christian Religions." *Nostra Aetate* and the way popes after the council have interpreted it raise the question of possibly admitting observers from other religions. As with Catholic laymen and laywomen, the new situation raises the further question of whether such potential presence should be limited to observing, without voice.

If some such expansion of membership takes place, the problem of an appropriate space becomes even more fraught. Moreover, the practicality of such large numbers gathered in a decision-making meeting is questionable. Active participation of each member is the ideal. At all three councils of the modern period, however, a relatively few bishops claimed the floor, while the rest sat and listened—or supposedly listened. Most meetings tend to follow that pattern, but the large scale of an ecumenical council compounds and exacerbates the problem. The number of participants present at Vatican II seems to be almost the limit.

A potential solution is a meeting of a more manageable number of bishops (and others), chosen or elected in an equitable way to represent different cultures and viewpoints, modeled somewhat on the Synods of Bishops that have met since Vatican II. Unlike those synods, however, which are by definition instruments of the Holy See with a strictly consultative role, the new body would need to conform to the teaching on episcopal collegiality of Vatican II and thus function in its relationship to the Holy See as have the councils. In other words, these meetings would not be instruments of the Holy See, just as councils are not such instruments, but are, as the traditional definition of councils has it, meetings of bishops gathered in Christ's name to make decisions binding on the church.

In that regard, we need to remember that the large percentage of eligible bishops who attended Vatican

II was not typical. At Nicaea, as mentioned, virtually no bishops came from the Latin church, and even at its peak the number at Trent represented only about a third of those eligible. Few would argue, however, that either of these cases is the ideal.

There are unquestionable advantages in the presence at a council of the full Catholic episcopacy. Although most bishops must sit passively during the meeting, they cast off their passivity when they vote. They in that way make their voices heard and provide for the church the litmus test of every issue under debate. The bishops who attend a council and vote at it acquire a sense of ownership of its decisions and thus serve as the most effective agents to ensure that decisions are communicated to the grassroots and are made effective. But how practical is such a meeting today?

Do the devices of the electronic technologies make it feasible and practical? Twenty years ago, few could have imagined the impact of smartphones, video conferencing, and the ever expanding resources provided by the Internet. These inventions have changed the way we conduct business. There is no reason to believe such developments are at an end. In some way or other, they might render moot the problem of size and location. The minimum that can be said with certainty at this point is that in some fashion or other they will have considerable impact on the next council or on the next meeting that replaces the pattern of councils.

Most people seem to assume that if and when there is another council it will meet in the Vatican. They anticipate a Vatican III. They are on solid ground. Of the thirteen ecumenical councils of the Western church, seven have met in Rome, and the last two met in the Vatican itself. In view of the increased authority Catholics have vested in the papacy in the last two centuries, the Vatican, the pope's home, now seems to be the appropriate place to hold a council.

Moreover, the practical advantages of meeting there are considerable. A full bureaucracy is already in place to prepare and organize the gathering. Aside from the basilica itself, the Vatican has a number of other spaces for the many smaller meetings of commissions and other bodies that a council necessarily entails. If space is lacking in the Vatican, it is amply available in the city of Rome. The city, accustomed to handling large crowds, can easily supply food and lodging for an even larger number of participants than at Vatican II.

Yet, councils are not predestined to meet in Rome. The first eight met in modern-day Turkey, and six of the Western councils met elsewhere in Europe. In the case of Trent, a non-Roman location was essential for the meeting to occur at all. When in the fall of 1870 it became clear that Vatican I could not continue in Rome after the city's seizure by the forces of the new Italian monarchy, a few leading prelates proposed that it move to Mechelen (Malines) in Belgium, an indication that even at that time an alternative to the Vatican was not assumed to be out of the question. Pius IX, however, refused to consider it.

The Vatican is located in Europe. Until relatively recently, the Catholic church was essentially a European church in that the majority of its members were in Europe, and its traditions and its problems were essentially European traditions and problems. Its missionaries were almost exclusively European, at least culturally, and they tended to impress European modes on the local churches they founded. In the past half-century that situation has changed.

Vatican Council II directed the church to face this new reality by greater accommodation to local cultures on a global scale. In the meantime, the importance of the Global South for the church has increased exponentially. That the next council should meet in Buenos Aires or in Nairobi is not unthinkable.

Do the advantages of delivering the preparation and organization of the council to the departments of the Roman curia outweigh the disadvantages? Are the advantages so great as almost to preclude the possibility of meeting elsewhere? That is not an idle question. The advantages are many and obvious. To construct a new organization for the task would require an enormous output of time and resources. But, given the new technologies, the Roman curia could possibly carry out an organizational role from a distance.

As mentioned in Chapter 3, however, a large majority of bishops at Vatican II fast came to the conclusion that the curia was an obstacle to overcome rather than a resource to ease the council's course. They deplored the decision that in the first place had handed to the curia the preparation of the council and then gave cardinals from the curia the key positions in the council's day-to-day operation.

Just because the relationship between the curia and the council was so unhappy at Vatican II does not necessarily mean that it by definition is unhappy. Had a few leading personnel of the curia been different at Vatican II, the outcome could well have been different. At Vatican I, for instance, the relationship was relatively untroubled—the curia was not the source of the frustration some of the bishops felt. Nonetheless, bureaucracies function according to norms and goals proper to themselves, and those norms and goals are not necessarily proper to meetings such as councils. To deliver the planning and organization of a meeting to an established bureaucracy almost inevitably imprints a certain form and set of assumptions on it even before it opens.

Even if the curia be given the task of preparing the council, should it not do so in a more inclusive way than at Vatican I and Vatican II? The Commission on the Lay Apostolate and the Secretariat for Promoting Christian Unity were the only noncurial bodies involved in forming the agenda for Vatican II, and the latter was the body responsible for some of the most important and characteristic documents of the council, documents that could hardly be imagined as coming from the curia.

Will there, then, be another ecumenical council? From the earliest times, church governance has been both collegial and hierarchical. Bishops gathered in council have been the quintessential expression of the collegial aspect. Aside from the governance bishops exercise over their own flocks, a pattern that was established in most cities by the early second century, the oldest institution of governance in the church is the council—local, provincial, and ecumenical.

Councils have met to deal with new problems and issues. They have met to deal with a changing world, even if the bishops present at the councils did not fully recognize that that was what they were doing. The world will certainly continue to change, and the church will have to deal with the changes. Councils have been the instrument for doing so when the changes were especially significant and challenging.

Will there be another ecumenical council? If tradition has any force in the Catholic church, the answer has to be a resounding affirmative. But, as the above considerations make clear, serious questions about its location, its membership, about how it might handle the large number of bishops and other potential participants, and about the precise form it might take hang in the air. Stay tuned.

Conclusion

THIS COMPARISON of Trent, Vatican I, and Vatican II has revealed a great deal about them and a great deal about the council phenomenon itself. Although the method of comparing councils is valid only when based on solid studies of each council in and for itself, it produces insights otherwise unavailable. This method has shown how the three councils relate or do not relate to one another, how certain basic issues recur and are handled in similar or different ways, and how some of those issues have been and will probably continue to be of concern. It has shown how those issues are both continuous and discontinuous with one another and with previous traditions.

Throughout the book, I have at least intimated that some issues, whether in the church or in other institutions, are not subject to final resolution. One of them is the relationship of tradition to innovation. It is the challenge of maintaining identity while adapting to new situations, the problem of remaining true to oneself without lapsing into irrelevance. For the church, this challenge is the result of being a historical institution, subject to the forces of the historical process. Such an institution is not an entity that can plow through the sea of history without being changed by the journey.

Another is the problem of the relationship between center and periphery, which for the councils is the relationship between the hierarchical and the collegial modes of church governance. Every institution needs firm guidance from the center and a firm hand at the helm. For the institution to remain vital, however, the authority of the center must be balanced by a periphery empowered to act on its own authority. If the balance between these poles is lost, it will almost inevitably result in either stagnation, on the one hand, disarray, on the other, or, in extreme cases, dissolution.

The comparison presented in this book has highlighted the problem of assessing the impact of councils. It has suggested how many factors must be taken into account and how intertwined the factors generally are. It has shown how dependent genuine assessment is upon the task the council sets itself. The task is, in turn, dependent on how the church understands itself and its role in the world. It is dependent on the council's implicit or explicit self-definition—that is, on how the council understands what it is doing.

By throwing light on the council phenomenon as such, the comparison has vindicated the tradition that bishops are the central, traditional, and determining participants. Although this has never been questioned, the comparison shows how the bishops' role has functioned in the three councils and how, despite many pressures, their role has remained central and determining. Their role constituted the first and most basic bond of continuity linking the three councils. It has proved the validity of the definition: Councils are meetings principally of bishops gathered in Christ's name to make decisions binding on the church. It made clear that among the bishops the bishop of Rome has without fail enjoyed a primacy.

The comparison has also revealed how important other participants in the councils have been. Whether physically present or not, the papal curia has been a participant. Since the thirteenth century, theologians have been indispensable for a council to function credibly. The laity, male and female, have been major players, even if they did not actually appear in the council chamber. The Other often set the councils on their course.

The comparison has shown how each council is unique and has features not shared by the others. In that regard, none stands out more clearly than Vatican II. The repercussions of its uniqueness are manifold. Supremely important among them, certainly, is the imperative to apply a different set of hermeneutical tools in interpreting it than were valid for previous councils. The first tool in that set is attention to the literary form the council adopted, because the form determined the goals the council hoped to achieve. Proper attention to the form will answer the most fundamental questions concerning the council: What was going on? What was the council trying to do?

The answers are in. Vatican II was not a legislative-judicial meeting whose primary purpose was securing public order in the church and isolating the church from outside contamination. It was, rather, a meeting to explore in depth the church's identity, to recall and make operative its deepest values, and to proclaim to the world its sublime vision for humanity. That is, in the last analysis, what Vatican II was all about. That is what it was trying to do. That is, therefore, the baseline for understanding what happened at Vatican II and for distinguishing it from all that went before.

Acknowledgments

At this point in the process of publishing a book, I am always struck by the generosity of friends and colleagues who have answered my sometimes desperate calls for help. This book has been no exception. As with my other books with Harvard University Press, Lindsay Waters, my editor, has been at my beck and call and has expertly guided the book through the publication process. His assistant, Joy Deng, has been extraordinarily helpful in answering my many queries and tending to my needs. Moreover, she went not the extra mile but many extra miles in volunteering to read the entire manuscript. She provided many important comments and criticisms, for which I am deeply grateful.

I am grateful to others who read my text or otherwise provided comments—John Borelli, Elizabeth Griffith Daniel, Justin Gronick, and Otto Hentz.

Acknowledgments

Leon Hooper, director of the Woodstock Theological Library at Georgetown, was as always quick to offer assistance, as was Amy Phillips, rare book cataloger at the library. My colleague Theresa Sanders almost daily extricated me from the traps into which I had fallen while trying to navigate the profound mysteries of the computer. Nelise Jeffrey, the office manager in the Theology Department, has come to my aid so often that I wonder she does not run in the opposite direction when she sees me coming. To one and all, profound thanks!

This volume reflects on and includes several short text excerpts from the books I have published with Harvard University Press about the three modern councils of the Catholic Church: *Trent, Vatican I,* and *What Happened at Vatican II.*

Index

Index

Index

Index